Self-Discovery Version

CHAINED
no
MORE

*A Journey of Healing for the
Adult Children of Divorce/Childhood Brokenness*

Robyn Besemann

CHAINED NO MORE
Breaking the Chains One Link at a Time
Written and Developed by Robyn Besemann

Edited by Stephanie McIver/Lynda Hodge
Cover Design by David Choates

This curriculum is not intended to be used as a replacement for therapists, counselors or other healthcare professionals. It is designed to be an additional resource to assist in the healing process. If further help is needed, please refer individuals to a psychologist or health-care professional.

For more information, contact:
Robyn Besemann
E-mail address: *robyn@robynbministries.com*
Web address: *robynbministries.com*

WestBow Press books may be ordered through booksellers or by contacting:

WestBow Press
A Division of Thomas Nelson
1663 Liberty Drive
Bloomington, IN 47403
www.westbowpress.com
1-(866) 928-1240

ISBN: 978-1-4908-1486-5 (sc)
ISBN: 978-1-4908-1487-2 (e)

Library of Congress Control Number: 2013921125

Printed in the United States of America

WestBow Press rev. date: 01/29/2014

TABLE OF CONTENTS

LINKS IN YOUR CHAIN

(Part One)

IDENTIFYING

CHAPTER ONE
Links In Your Chain (Part One)
Beginning The Journey

Are you struggling with issues of trust, abandonment, betrayal, anger or depression? Could it be that these issues might have begun with the separation/divorce of your parents? Could they possibly have come from other childhood brokenness that you have experienced?

Do you find it difficult to have a healthy, committed relationship? Do you find it hard to solve feelings of low self-worth, and do you feel as if you have to please everyone in your life?

Welcome to "Chained No More", a self-discovery book for the adult children of divorce to explore the many issues and effects their parents' separation/divorce have had on them in their adult life. If you have experienced other childhood brokenness and are seeking to break those chains, you will be able to adjust the "Chained No More" questions to fit your particular experiences.

It would be easier, as an adult child of divorce, to not "open that box" again and just go on with everyday life; however, you may have found that feelings of anger, depression, betrayal, abandonment, fear and mistrust, etc. keep coming up throughout your life. You may have experienced the breakup of multiple relationships and are puzzled about the reasons why they failed. Have you asked yourself "What's wrong with me?"

It is important to see where feelings come from so you can recognize them, address them, and see the power they have had over you (occasionally or often). By utilizing the practical tools you will learn from this material, you will find healing from these feelings and hopefully be able to move forward without the chains they have placed upon you. You will learn things about yourself that may surprise you. You are worth the time and effort this important process will take, so please do not hurry through it.

Within this process of healing, it is important for you to be completely honest with the details of your experiences and how you feel about them. The more open you are and the more work you put into this, the more benefits you will experience. You are on a journey of self-discovery and healing. Can you take a chance and be purely honest?

This study of discovery is not something that is meant to disrespect your parents or your family in any way. It is, however, a means to see how your childhood experiences have played a part in your adult life and why you continue to struggle for answers.

The statistics are very high for divorce in our country and our world. Many couples in our present society don't marry at all, but still have children. You are not the only one feeling what you feel and this may be the first time you have allowed yourself to be honest about it. You may be one who likes to share with many people, get their perspective, and hope for their approval or you may be one who keeps everything inside. It is important within this journey to keep it private, for the time being, as you explore. If you share with others, you may be influenced to think a different way than you actually do, or it could cause more family drama. Right now, keep it between you, the Lord and the pages of this book and see where this journey of healing leads.

Please find adequate time alone and without distractions for your time in "Chained No More". Allow yourself at least 3 days between chapters to really absorb what you have discovered. This is not a quick fix, but a journey. Take your time to answer the questions as honestly as you can, and dig deep. Begin each session by asking the Lord to open your eyes, your mind, and your heart to what He has for you on this journey. Are you ready?

Breanna, 24, was a college student trying to work toward her master's degree. Her childhood was messy with siblings in jail, parents who were in constant chaos and violence surrounding her. She vowed she was going to be the first one in her family to complete college and she spent almost every waking minute in front of the computer screen or books. Her social life was very limited and her interactions with guys were few and far between. She said that she was just too busy to have a social life at that point.

On the weekends, her roommates would invite her to the football games, out for pizza with large groups, attend singles' events at their church and sometimes even go out of town for the weekend. Sadly, Breanna declined their offers and instead, she chose to head to the library on campus or stay in her dorm room to study for the next exam. She was totally focused on her long-term goals.

One day, her friend, Sadie asked her to coffee and they began to talk about relationships they had experienced. Breanna shared that there was one boy in high school she dated for awhile, but that relationship only lasted for about six months. Most of the guys in her school were more interested in drinking, having sex, and trying drugs, so she stayed clear of them. Sadie was curious and asked, "There *are* good guys out there too, Breanna. Why haven't you had more boyfriends? You are 24, Girl!"

Breanna thought for a moment, sighed and said, "Most of the guys I knew in high school were in gangs and that was their life. I really don't trust guys at all. That one boyfriend I did have in high school broke up with me because he liked another girl. At least that is what I was told by a couple of friends. This is what happened to my mom and dad too! Dad had an affair with another woman and left my mom and us kids. We were even homeless for eight months and had to live in a shelter! I will *never* be able to forgive him or completely trust a man again, so I would rather be alone than get hurt like my mom. She *still* hasn't gotten over it! I am going to make something of myself and I will do it alone!"

Do you see how her opinion of men was based on what happened with her mom and dad? That was one of the most devastating experiences of her life and she based her thoughts of all men on that *one* experience.

This is what "*Chained No More*" is all about: To break those chains that may have covered you and you have been dragging behind you for years while jading your opinions, beliefs and decisions. Just because your parents separated/divorced does not mean that you are predestined to experience your own divorce, even though statistics show that the majority of adult children of divorce do. However, maybe you have already been divorced once or multiple times. One of the biggest goals of "*Chained No More*" is to help break the pattern of divorce in families through healing and practical tools.

Statistics of divorce, according to divorcerate.org and Marriage Success Secrets, are as follows:

- 41% of first marriages will end in divorce
- 60% of second marriages will end in divorce
- 73% of subsequent marriages will end in divorce
- 50% of American children will witness the divorce of their parents by age 18
- 50% of children will also witness their parents' second divorce
- 3 million unmarried couples are living together in the USA, an 80% increase since 1980. Note: Higher breakup rate than married couples
- 49% of children in our country live without a father in the home.
- 21.8 million children are living in single-parent households

What has happened to our society and the importance of a healthy family? How did this happen? Pause for a moment. What are your thoughts on this? This is the third generation of heavy divorce stats in which divorce seems to be an option, yet we make the same vows at a wedding. "...better or worse, richer or poorer, in sickness and in health, forsaking all others, for as long as we both shall live." *Really*? Those words are easy to say; however, but many times, we are not willing to put in the work to make them "stick", are we?

Those important vows don't include all the damage from childhood or previous issues. They don't take into account the fear a child of divorce carries into a supposedly lifetime commitment. It seems like vows nowadays could be, "...for better or until you tick me off, for richer or until you lose your job or bills began to mount up, in sickness but not catastrophic illness/injury, forsaking all others unless they are better than you, for as long as we get along."

Beginning today, take your time as you explore the issues that may have come from your own parents' separation/divorce and the losses you have had because of those experiences and other childhood brokenness. "Chained No More" will help you begin to identify the links of the chains that may have been keeping you from being free to be all you were meant to be. May God bless you and guide you as you journey through this study, and may you sense His presence in every chapter. Begin with Chapter 1 in the workbook section of this book.

"May the Lord direct your hearts into God's love and Christ's perseverance." II Thessalonians 3:5

LINKS IN YOUR CHAIN
(Part Two)

IDENTIFYING

CHAPTER TWO
Links In Your Chain (Part Two)
Taking A Trip Back

You have opened the door to what could be a turning point in your life. The previous chapter may have caused you to see things you had forgotten about or brought emotions closer to the surface as you saw the effects of your parents' separation/divorce and other childhood brokenness. Ask the Lord to open your heart and soul so He can bring you healing from the hurt of that and other painful experiences and move you toward freedom to be the best you can be.

In this chapter, you will be exploring the actual experience of your parents' separation/divorce and other experiences. It will bring you back to the details, emotions, and effects of them on various parts of your life at the time. There is also an alternate page if your parents didn't separate/divorce but you have suffered other trauma.

Take a moment to answer each of the following questions.

- How old were you when your parents split up or when you suffered other trauma?
- Were you a little child, a teenager or even older?
- Did you feel sadder or angrier about it?
- Do you remember the tension and stress of it?
- Do you remember where you were?
- When the divorce of your parents took place, were you happy because there would be no more fighting or abuse?
- Did you even know both or one of your parents or were they gone before you were old enough to remember? Maybe your parents were never married at all. Every story is different.
- Were you in foster care or adopted? How has that affected you?

All of these questions may not be pleasant to think about, but they are necessary to take the next step toward healing. They can show you the power that childhood experiences have had over you for a long time. They can also show you how much you have tucked away from your memory to cope with your everyday life. What three words would you use to describe your childhood? Write them here. _____

Another question...did you think divorce would ever happen to you in your marriage? Did it? Do you see any similarities of your marriage(s) or relationship(s) and your parents' marriage(s) or relationship(s)? Did you and your spouse/partner handle your own breakups the same way as your parents? Think deeply about it. Look for the chains.

What do you think it takes to have a healthy, long-lasting marriage/relationship? Pause and think about this. Do you think it is possible for you? Why or why not?

You may have had parents who did not separate/divorce, but maybe they should have with all the fighting and arguing they did. You may not have seen a healthy marriage and really don't understand how two people can have a successful and loving, long term marital relationship. We will explore marriage in depth in a later chapter, but for now, let's move on.

Jason and Marianne met on a blind date when they were in their early 20s and it seemed like everything clicked. They could talk about anything, including the fact that both of their parents divorced when they were younger. Each had suffered abuse at varying levels in their childhood. Jason's dad was an alcoholic and Marianne thought her mom also drank too much sometimes. This young couple seemed like peanut butter and jelly or chips and salsa, so marriage seemed to be their future.

Jason and Marianne got married in a beautiful ceremony on the beach at sunset and vowed their love and devotion to each other in front of family and friends. This was a marriage that would last forever, for sure.

Four years into the marriage, Jason lost his job. Marianne seemed to be losing interest in having a close relationship with him and she began to spend more time with the children and their activities. Jason hung out with his friends fixing up old cars and watching just about every sports event on his big screen TV that he could. Oh, the bills somehow got paid, the kids got to their activities, and annual holidays usually focused on the children, but the love connection between Jason and Marianne was slowly breaking. They were emotionally detaching.

One day, Jason found Marianne crying in the kitchen and asked her what the problem was. She said, "I don't feel married anymore! I just feel like all I do is pick up after you and the kids and run them around! All we seem to do lately is argue and your drinking is getting out of control, Jason. The kids get scared when you are drunk sometimes and so do I. I don't know what to do! Don't you love me anymore? Do you want a divorce? I am miserable. Aren't you? Maybe we should go to counseling."

Jason replied, "I don't feel married either, but there is no way that I am going to go tell someone our problems in a fancy office! Seriously! It's no wonder I drink a little too much. If you didn't spend so much time with the kids, maybe there would be more time for us!" Marianne bristled and replied, "If *someone* would help me around here and spend more time with the kids and me, maybe we *would* have more time together! You are just like your dad!"

The fight was on, lasted over an hour and both of them began to consider calling it quits. They eventually did divorce, just like their parents, and dragged their precious children through exactly what they had both been dragged through as kids. Chains.

You may have had parents who fought, either verbally, physically or both, or you may have had parents who kept their fights to themselves and kept you out of it. When your parents argued, what did you do as a kid? Did you go hide in the closet, lay on the bed in your room with a pillow over your head, turn music up really loud, or leave the house? Perhaps you stayed there and tried to be the peacemaker or defend one parent or the other. Maybe you screamed for your parents to stop fighting or just stood there and cried. Were the police involved? What were you feeling, and how do you feel now as you remember it?

When children hear their parents argue, they have feelings of great insecurity. They feel like they have no control and they don't know whose side to stand on. Loyalty issues can become huge! Sometimes parents fight about the child and then the child feels guilty. They may feel they are the cause of the conflict and eventually even the reason for the divorce. Children carry a lot of the burden and are not mature or wise enough to distinguish properly between right and wrong, who is at fault or what the next steps should be. They are left feeling helpless, hopeless, and their identity has shattered just like their family. The truth is...no matter if children were told the divorce was their fault or not, a child is *never* to blame. That was between two adults and it was their decision and their ability or inability to "work it out". It is certainly not the child's.

Another issue that can leave a child feeling helpless is not knowing the *true* reason for the separation/divorce. Parents may give their child a reason for the separation or divorce such as "We just don't get along anymore", "Mommy and Daddy just don't love each other anymore" or "this marriage didn't work out". Many children then form the fear that if their parents get mad at them, they may stop loving this hurting child and walk away from *them* too. They may begin to question love and security altogether. These issues become deeper with each remarriage of their parent and they will lose respect for them. So begins the cycle of fear, abandonment and a jaded sense of security. What do love, vows and commitment really mean anyway? Do you see how the family chains continue generation after generation?

Parents trying to "keep the child out of it", many times opt to keep the details from the child such as the reason for the divorce, what the child custody issues are, how extended family members are getting involved, the possibility of moving, financial issues, etc. Other parents feel they need to tell the children almost everything, whether they are old enough to absorb it or not.

Many times, parents will talk to their child derogatorily about their other parent and blame them for the entire divorce. The child loves both parents and is torn in the middle. They learn to keep secrets, lie, keep information from parents and struggle to keep all of it straight. What a horrible place to be as a child! It truly is an ugly battlefield. The kids pay the highest price. All of these experiences stop the child from "just being a kid" and they are forced to grow up much faster than is healthy for them. These issues will certainly follow the child throughout their adult life and relationships if not addressed and healed from.

You might recognize some of this behavior in the way you have handled your own separation/divorce and how it may have affected your own children. The damage has been done, but it can be very healing to sincerely and humbly apologize to your kids for your part in the situation no matter how long ago your divorce/separation happened.

You may have found that your behavior began to change when you were going through the trauma of your parents' separation/divorce. Your anger may have clouded your judgment and led you to fight, yell, abuse others or pets and not accept authority. Why would you trust an adult when the ones closest to you obliterated your life? Your grades at school may have taken a dive because you couldn't concentrate on anything but the family trauma. This may have caused you to lose confidence in your intelligence and ability to do well in school. This could have been the beginning of giving up and settling for less education or not applying for better jobs. Does this sound familiar to you? It is important to look at the "whys behind the whats" in your life decisions so you can begin to break negative patterns.

It is of utmost importance for you to realize that no matter what you have experienced, you don't have to define yourself by it. Even if you have been through abuse, isolation or abandonment, abortion, incarceration, bad choices, multiple sexual partners, or the horrid damage from your parents' separation/divorce (or your own), *God made you, knows you, sees you, and He loves and accepts you. If you just sat there and breathed, He would love you beyond your understanding. Yes, you!*

You may not feel that right now. You may not feel worthy of such unconditional love. None of us deserves the Lord's deep love and care, but His arms are open wide to all of us, no matter what our past includes. Hopefully, through this journey, you will be able to base your self-worth on *His* amazing love for you and not what any person or circumstance has ever told you. This study will not "beat you over the head with the Bible", but will consistently lead you to His Word for truth that will overshadow the lies, betrayal and hurt from your past.

Truth is, first of all, a quality that belongs to God, to Christ and to the Holy Spirit. God wants truth developed in us. We must *seek* it, *speak* it, *walk* in it, *live* by it and *worship* in it, because only *then* will we *truly be free.*

"Then you will know the truth and the truth will set you free." John 8:32

Go to Chapter 2 in the workbook and explore how the separation/divorce of your parents and other childhood experiences have affected areas in your life. As you see the possible origin of issues and losses, thank the Lord that He is opening your eyes, mind, and heart and beginning the process of understanding and healing.

UNDERSTANDING THE LINKS

CONNECTIONS

CHAPTER THREE
Understanding The Links
The Chain Of Grief

Whether the separation/divorce of your parents or other trauma was last year or 30 years ago, the grief you felt and may still feel is real. Just when you think you are "over it", some experience, smell, sound or touch may bring it all back to you.

You have every right to grieve over the horrible pain you have had or may still be feeling. Divorce may be beyond painful and can affect most every area of your life; your relationships, self-worth, security, decision-making, habits, addictions, issues of faith, etc.

Many times, children of divorce walk through family trauma and seem like they are fine. They try very hard to let people, including their parents, know that they will be fine and it doesn't affect them that much. They may even believe that themselves. What can happen is that the emotional damage of their family's breakup often will surface when they are in their 20s, when they become involved in significant relationships. This is called "the sleeper effect". Issues of trust, abandonment, betrayal and lack of commitment can rear their ugly heads and they don't know why. Looking back at their past, they begin to see where these issues originated from.

Grief can come from the death of someone we love, a divorce or separation, loss of a job, or any number of other situations. Grief can cycle through over a matter of months or can last for years on end, if we don't work through it and do what we need to by forgiving and coming to acceptance. Both of these are a process and not just a choice. It takes time and effort to work through them honestly and diligently. This process can be very painful, but have life-changing results.

When the family trauma initially happens, most of the time, we can't believe it happened. "There is no way that my parents are splitting up. They love us too much to ruin our family!" Sound familiar? When someone dies, especially if it was a sudden death, we are unable to absorb the news and think it might be a mistake. The shock is too great.

Definition of denial: "A negotiation in logic or a refusal to admit the truth or reality." Denial is a protective emotion that shields us from pain. Denial can mean anything from avoiding the subject of the divorce to focusing on others, to always keeping busy and never slowing down enough to feel or talk. We put it in a little box and stuff it away, hoping it will just "go away".

One rainy spring night 16-year-old Tyler's mom and dad asked him to come down to the living room so they could talk to him. He thought, "Uh oh, what did I do now?" When he walked into the room, he noticed that neither parent was smiling. Actually, come to think of it, it had been a long time since he had seen smiles in the house.

Tyler sat down on one end of the couch and waited to get scolded for something else. His father cleared his throat and then said, "Son, your mom and I have something we need to tell you. We have had a lot of problems lately. I am sure you may have noticed that there has been a lot of tension in the last several months. Your mom and I think it is best if we separate and probably get a divorce."

Tyler's world stopped in that moment and it seemed like everything went blank. He looked at his mom, who was crying, then back at his dad. The first thing that came out of his mouth was, "Are you kidding me?! I knew you guys were having trouble, but you can't be serious! Mom, is this what *you* want? *Really*? Don't I mean anything at all to you guys?! You always tell me to work my problems out. Why don't *you*?"

His mind was spinning, his heart was racing, anger began to rise and tears began to well up in his eyes. Both parents talked for a bit and explained how it would work with his dad moving out and how mom was going to go look for a better job and that everything would work out. Tyler barely could focus on what they were saying, but he could see that they had thought this whole thing out without his input and it was about to shatter everything in his life. He never thought this would happen to him. There just *had* to be a way to change their minds and reverse this horrible decision.

For the next few weeks, Tyler refused to talk about the divorce and thought that if he left his parents alone, they would work out their problems and his dad would move back in. Tyler's parents divorced six months later. Tyler's grades began to drop, and he stayed in his room most of the time. His life had just been changed forever. What could he have done? Was it his fault? What would happen now?

When parents divorce, children just can't absorb the situation. They can't hide under a blanket or isolate themselves in a closet and make it go away. They have no control over this devastation of dreams of a happy, healthy family. At first, it is just easier to deny it is happening.

Bargaining can be the next step many times for children. "If I clean my room and do all my chores, maybe mommy and daddy will stop fighting about me and not get a divorce." "If I play soccer really well, maybe Daddy will come to my game and they can sit by each other and make up." "If we all sit down as a family and watch a funny movie and eat popcorn like we used to, maybe Mom and Dad will see the mistake they are making."

Children will do most anything to get their parents back together. They feel that if their parents love them enough, they will try to reconcile and everything will be okay. Time after time, children are disappointed when their parents talk without fighting, but then walk away again and again. Their expectations are dashed repeatedly and after awhile, they just stop hoping.

Definition of bargaining: "Testing whether something is open to negotiation or may be reversible." Bargaining for the child of divorce could have included trying to get parents to seek help for their marriage, attempting to be a peacemaker or mediator between parents, or causing problems so parents would focus on the child and not their relationship issues. Maybe you tried some of these things when you were experiencing the family crisis.

Children, in general, have a way of bargaining for a lot of things and many times they are successful as their parents give in to their requests/demands. If a parent eventually gives in, the child will learn how far they will have to go next time to get their way. Maybe they will have to yell or scream a little longer, maybe they will have to cry or throw a tantrum or maybe they will have to try and get another answer from their other parent. They will do what it takes to get what they want.

Now, all of a sudden, the child does not have any control over their parents' decision to separate/divorce. They may get mad, yell and scream, or fall apart in tears. They have every right to feel the pain they do, but *nothing* they do will make a difference this time.

It is at this point that kids will try different ways to make their parents change their mind. There just HAS to be something they can do to turn this family trauma around! How sad that a child feels they need to control the decisions of their parents, especially if they feel the divorce/separation is their fault.

Neither denial nor bargaining could work, because the issue of divorce was between your parents. Nothing you could say or do would ultimately keep them together. It was not your fault, nor was it your problem to fix. You probably still don't know all the issues between your parents and you don't know all that happened behind closed doors. That is why it didn't make sense.

Your parent(s) may have even told you that it was all or partially your fault that they were getting a divorce and you have carried that guilt and shame for a long time. There are many elderly adults who still carry that burden and may carry it to their graves. Your parents were the ones who made the decision to separate/divorce, have an affair, walk away, abuse, etc. Chances are they each brought their own hurts and issues into their marriage in the first place. Those were *not* your decisions and there was *nothing* you could have done about it. You are only responsible for your own actions and decisions.

This is where trust in God for each step of this journey should begin. He sees you and He knows you. He knew all of the challenges you would have in your life as well as the outcome. Many times, kids get mad at God and blame Him for their parents' divorce. Did you or do you now blame Him today for the hurts in your life? Be honest. He knows and He understands.

God didn't cause the divorce or other trauma, but, for some reason, He allowed it. Your parents had a free will just like you do. We all make decisions that are not according to His perfect plan for us and then we blame Him for the outcome. Many times we pray and pray and pray and ask God for things and when we don't see Him answer the way we want, we ask ourselves, "What's the point?" Sound familiar?

Many of us use God like a candy store. "God, please give me three of those and a dozen of those and six of those." "If You give me that, I will give You this." Other times, we pray to Him like He is the complaint department or a whipping post. Sometimes we pray when we don't even have a relationship with Him and there are also times when we may treat Him like a close friend or the Almighty God He is.

The way we pray to the Lord is an indication of how much we trust Him, love Him and the relationship we have with Him. Praying is just talking to God. It isn't about how fancy you pray, or saying just the right words; it is about honest and open communication. He is the Almighty God, however, He wants to hear what is on your heart, hear your hurts, and what you are grateful for. In doing so, you are building a closer connection and relationship with Him. It is just between you and Him. Even when you may be feeling angry with Him for letting all of the trauma happen to you, He wants to connect with you. Our trust in God and His care for us is important, especially when there are trials.

Trust is something that is earned and it is not a right. From the moment you were born, you had to trust your parent(s) to clothe you and feed you, to meet your every need. One day, trust was broken in a big way when your parents separated/divorced. Other situations may have shattered your ability to trust as well, and here you sit filled with issues that have held you back from being the best you can be.

Maybe you lost your trust in people in general, or in God, or even believing in love and marriage. Your dream for a healthy family was shattered. Maybe you didn't know who to trust. Maybe your mom said one thing and your dad said another. Who do you believe? Eventually, you couldn't deny the divorce or try to manipulate your way out of it. It was reality!

We begin this journey toward healing by understanding the Chain of Grief. Although there are many more emotions you felt or may still be feeling, we have chosen the Chain of Grief for "Chained No More". Dig deep about how you feel or felt as you progress through the chapters and explore the Chain of Grief in Chapter 3 in the workbook.

"Let us hold unswervingly to the hope we profess, for He who promised is faithful." Hebrews 10:23

"Teach me Your way, O Lord, and I will walk in Your truth; give me an undivided heart, that I may fear Your name." Psalm 86:11

POWER OF THE CHAIN

"His divine power has given us everything we need for life and godliness through our knowledge of Him who called us by His own glory and goodness, through these He has given us His very great and precious promises, so that through them, you may participate in the divine nature and escape the corruption in the world caused by evil desires" (2 Peter 1:3–4).

CHAPTER FOUR
Power Of The Chain
Family Patterns And Their Effects

Have you ever found yourself sounding like your mom or your dad? How about looking in the mirror and seeing a disturbing resemblance to someone in your family? Maybe, in an argument with someone, they spewed out, "You are acting just...like...your...dad!"

The way we butter our bread, make our beds, bite our nails, negotiate when buying a car, wear our hair, yell at the dog, or any number of other actions can show a family pattern. Holiday traditions, religious practices, brands of cars, or favorite recipes can show family patterns as well.

Family patterns can be positive and give us a feeling of belonging or can be quite negative and give us a feeling of helplessness or distaste. We may get angry at ourselves because we see that we "are just...like...your...dad (or mom)". We may also feel proud when someone tells us, "I see that you are a hard worker just...like...your...dad (or mom).

The same is true about the pattern of divorce in our families. This is the third generation of heavy divorce in our country and your family may have a number of divorces going back many years. This may also be said of abuse or addiction patterns in families. It is important, within this *"Chained No More"* journey to look back and see where your current attitudes and issues may have come from so you can see the power they have had on you.

We are all a product of our parenting, good or bad. Some of us had caring parents, whether they divorced or not. Some of us had abusive parents or neglectful parents. There is nothing you or anyone else can do to change that now, but it is important to explore the parenting you had and how it has affected you up to this point in your life. When you do that, you can make the choice to continue those patterns or break the chains for generations ahead. You no longer have to sweep it under the carpet and say, "That's just how I am".

What is your idea of a "perfect parent"? Would your description include a parent who spent time with you, talked with you and not at you? A parent who was kind and caring? A parent, who taught and trained you for your adult life, respected you, was honest with you, valued your family and laughed with you? Many of us have had that kind of parent, but many of us have not. Many of us were that type of parent to our own kids, but many of us were not.

Once again, you may have had a parent or parents, who were not available to you, or abused you, neglected you, and never made you feel you had much value at all. It is common for children to define themselves by what their parents told them or did to them negatively and just resign to the fact that they will do the same thing. *You do not have to define yourself by what happened to you as a child, whether it is divorce, abuse, putdowns or anything else.* Read that last sentence again. Now, read it out loud, but replace "you, yourself and you" with "I, myself, and me".

Just because your parent had an affair, was abusive, an alcoholic, put in jail, was lazy or any other negative behavior, does not mean you are destined for the same thing. On the other hand, if your parents loved, cared, nurtured and provided for you, you can transfer that kind of parenting forward to your children and beyond, as well. It is possible to break the patterns and make the life of your family a much healthier experience than what you lived.

As you explore the patterns in your family, be encouraged, not discouraged. You are now on a path of healing and freedom. This is the next step toward a much more positive future where you can make a difference in a positive way. Even if someone told you that you would amount to nothing or that you were a loser or any number of other horrible putdowns, *it is not true.* "All things are possible to them who love God." God's Word is bigger than any human being's words or actions, right?

"Can you keep a secret?" "Can I trust you?" "Don't tell your mom/dad about this." "You can tell me what your dad did this past weekend. I won't say anything." Does this sound familiar?

In a child's mind, the stakes are extraordinarily high if they should somehow slip up and break a confidence or forget what secret to keep. It could mean that their parents will have another fight or make sure their parents won't get back together as the child had hoped.

Many kids of divorce are expected to keep secrets between their parents and also lie about what the "other parent" is doing. Kids are put right in the middle and taught at an early age how to be untruthful, spy on others, and develop an overall sense of mistrust. Sometimes, communication is very closed and there are secrets and very little openness in a family.

In the case of abuse, kids are controlled and are commanded not to tell anyone or something terrible will happen to them or someone they love. They have no other choice but to keep the secret and continue to suffer the damage done to them. These children will usually shrink into a world of pain and isolation, riddled by guilt and shame.

Loyalty issues are huge with kids of divorce (ie. "Who should I go to live with?" "What if I tell Dad that Mom has a boyfriend?" "What if I really like Dad's new 'friend'"? "Will that hurt Mom's feelings?"). On and on and on....

Even today, you may still be expected to play this game between your parents and you don't know how to get off of their battlefield. First of all, do you want to? Are you tired of going back and forth, feeling like a pinball machine and trying to remember what you told each of them or what they told you? Maybe you like being "in the loop" by going back and forth between your parents, but you find yourself feeling angry and bitter at times. In trying to be the peacemaker, you may, in fact, be enabling them to hurt each other and you. Take a moment to think about the relationship you have with each of your parents and about where you might step back.

It is important, for your own healing as well as peace in your family, you talk to each of your parents about stepping off their battlefield and not being a part of it anymore. You might say something like, "Mom/Dad, I have been going between both of you for a long time. It is time that I step off your battlefield and let you deal with your own issues together, if you care to. I will not be keeping secrets for either of you, lying for you or spying on the other one for you anymore. I love you both and I want to be free to do that." How would that feel if you said it calmly but firmly as an adult now?

What they choose to do with their relationship from then on is up to the two of them. Maybe they would realize they need to resolve their own issues instead of relying on you to be their mediator. Maybe they would just decide it isn't worth it anymore and completely separate. In stepping off their battlefield and not being manipulated anymore, you have no more responsibility for that and you can move forward and break that link in your chain. The challenge will probably be your consistency in your decision and not being caught up in their drama again.

Shayla, an energetic 8-year-old, was devastated when her mommy and daddy decided to separate. Daddy moved out to another apartment with his "friend" and Mommy, Shayla and her brother, Eric, moved to a duplex across town. Shayla and Eric got to go to Daddy's house every other weekend and on Wednesdays after school. It was fun to be at Daddy's because he had an aboveground pool and they would spend hours swimming. He also got a new fancy truck and took them on long rides in the country to get ice cream and see the farm animals.

Life was different at Mommy's house. There wasn't a lot of laughing or having fun together. Mommy was always tired and they just didn't have the money to go to the movies or buy new toys. Shayla's favorite thing to do with Mommy was to cuddle in her big bed and watch TV. Mommy had a new "friend" now and she seemed to be a little happier, which made Shayla happy.

It seemed like every single time Shayla and Eric arrived at Mommy's or Daddy's house for a visit, she was interrogated with a long line of questions. Mommy would ask, "What did your Daddy and his girlfriend do? Do they kiss in front of you?" "Where did he get the money for that truck? We don't even have enough money for me to get our car *fixed*!" Daddy would ask, "What does your mom do with the money I give her? Does she get her hair or nails done? She is supposed to spend it on you and Eric." "If she is not going to let you go for that week in March, then I am going to pay her less that month. See how she likes that!" All of this made Shayla feel like a dollar bill and not worth much more than that.

Both of them hurt Shayla deeply by saying, "Well, who do you love more, your mommy/daddy or me?" And so the battle raged on for this little girl and her brother. She found out that if she just kept her mouth shut or lied, it kept her from the arguments that came from these interrogations. Such pressure and damage for a little 8-year-old girl!

If little Shayla looked back, she may have felt that the separation of her parents was her fault. She may have heard her parents fighting over her, whether it was her behavior, ballet schedule, how much money they should "pay" for her or even how she talked back to her mom.

Many children think that for some reason, their parents' separation/divorce was partially or entirely their fault. Some kids only hear one side of the story or they haven't been told the true reason for the divorce until much later in life. Usually, they will hear a biased account of what happened and the child stands between them in confusion. Again, the truth is that there is nothing you could have done that would have prevented your parents' separation/divorce, as sad as that is. It was their choice and their choice alone. Yes, it had a profound impact on your life, but you had no choice in it. Hopefully, you will accept this fact and that the workbook page called, "It's Not My Fault" will help solidify what is in your control and what is not.

It is important to evaluate where your attitudes, beliefs, actions, and feelings come from. Again, this is not meant to blame or disrespect your parents, but it is a tool to understand the issues you have in your life and how they may relate back to your childhood and had such power over you. Your parents had or have their own issues they can explore. However, you need to dig deep to discover your own issues. It may just open the door to healing for you!

"Open my eyes that I may see glimpses of truth Thou hast for me..."

Meditate on the following scriptures before going to Chapter 4 in the workbook.

"Turn my eyes away from worthless things; preserve my life according to Your Word." Psalm 119:37

"By His divine power, God has given us everything we need for living a godly life. We have received all of this by coming to know Him, the One who called us to Himself by means of His marvelous glory and excellence. And because of His glory and excellence, He has given us great and precious promises. These are the promises that enable you to share His divine nature and escape the world's corruption caused by human desires." II Peter 1:3-4

Chapter Five

GRIP OF THE CHAIN

ANGER

example we have been given. However, it is never too late to evaluate the reason for our anger, the emotions behind it and the effects others' anger has had on us. We can also explore how our anger has affected others over the years. Is this the time for you to reach out for healing for the anger you hold?

In the Chapter 5 workbook pages, you will be able to explore the subject of anger, your experience with anger and what the Lord God says about it in His Word. Take a deep breath and let's get to work.

UNDER THE GRIP OF THE CHAIN

WHAT'S REALLY GOING ON?

CHAPTER SIX
Under The Grip Of The Chain
Exploring What Is Behind Anger

There are literally hundreds of emotions we feel throughout our lives. Many times, we generally label them as only a few: angry, happy, sad, confused, frustrated, etc. In fact, if we thought about it, we could probably think of an emotion beginning with every letter of the alphabet. Why don't you try that now? Take a piece of paper, write the alphabet down the side of the page and write an emotion beginning with each letter. This is not as easy as it sounds.

When we look deeper, we can identify these emotions for what they truly are and then deal with them in a more honest and open way (ie. *anger* because someone cancelled on us, could mean we are really *disappointed*, or feeling *lonely* or *abandoned*). In this example, anger may cause us to ignore the person who let us down, write them off or blow up at them, whereas, realizing our disappointment/loneliness/abandonment might cause us to try to resolve it.

Another way we "deal" with emotions is to just put them aside, ignore them and try to move on. We may say that the person who hurt us is not worth it or we don't want to cause more problems. We may think we just have to "forgive and forget", but what happens is that it prevents us from dealing with it, resolving the conflict, and usually have resentment resurface later. Over years of not resolving the issue, it can cause us to have a root of bitterness that we can never be free of.

Let's look at some examples of how we get angry, and how anger is an "umbrella emotion" for what we are really feeling inside.

1) Your boss calls you into his office and tells you that he is going to have to cut your hours because he has been told that you have not been carrying your weight, and the company is trying to cut down on costs.

   Your blood begins to boil because you know who told him that; it was your supervisor who has a grudge against you because you made him look inferior once.

   LOOK DEEPER: Could you be feeling *frustration*, like an *injustice* has been done, *scared* because your budget is already stretched too far, and *embarrassed* because you look bad to your boss? Maybe this has happened to you before.

   Your first reaction after shock would probably be one of anger and could spin you into words and actions of anger, as well as prevent you from choosing a healthy way of communicating and reaching some understanding and resolution.

2) As a child, your parents tell you they were going to separate and might be getting a divorce. Daddy is going to move into an apartment and you, your mom and sisters are going to have to move into a smaller house.

   You begin to feel the tears well up in your eyes and your whole body begins to feel tight. Last week, when your parents had another fight, you asked your mom if they were going to get a divorce and she said, "Of course not, we will work it out." Now, they are telling you that your entire life is going to fall apart. You begin to get mad and begin to scream, *"But you promised you would work it out!"*

   LOOK DEEPER: Could you have been feeling *scared* because you didn't know what was going to happen next (where would you live, would you ever see your dad, what happens on your birthday, etc.?), *betrayed* because Mom said they would "work it out", *abandoned* because Daddy was leaving and would not be around, or feeling like you were completely *out of control* and you had no choice in this?

After the shock and disbelief of the announcement from your parents, you may have reacted in anger by running to your room in tears or just sitting there stone-faced. Depending on their age, children have not developed skills to communicate effectively especially in this situation. They just react and don't think about the consequences. Sound familiar?

Another way that we can "deal with" difficult situations is to worry. Oh, we worry about the economy, whether our kids will do well in life, whether our spouse really loves us as much as they say they do, our health, politics, where we are going to get our next meal, if we are safe, if we are ever going to get out of this situation/relationship, etc. etc. etc. We can even worry about being worried, for heaven's sake! Worry causes stress, stress causes health problems and a myriad of other issues.

Do you realize that every single moment that we worry, we are saying to God, "I don't trust You with my life. You can't handle all I go through. Your promises are not true for me"?

God's promises are, "I will never leave you nor forsake you." "Behold, I am with you always even unto the end of the age." "Be still and know that I AM GOD." The list of His promises goes on and on and they are for *you* every single hour of every single day of every single year of your life and for all eternity. Later in this study, you will see how much He really loves, treasures and surrounds you. He is worthy of our trust and faith.

In this chapter, we are going to look at the many emotions that could be connected with the separation/or divorce of your parents and other childhood brokenness. This won't be easy as you dig deeper into how you feel, but it is a necessary step to walk closer to healing. It may be that you have turned your emotions off so you can get through every day. You may not be in touch with your emotions, because it is safer that way, yet you try to have relationships that don't ever seem to work out. It is virtually impossible to have a healthy, long-lasting marriage/relationship if you don't have an emotional connection.

It would be easier to just be angry, react or hold it in, but it is important for you to not continue to bury emotions. Allow them to come to the surface so they can be dealt with and healed. It is well worth the time, fear and uncomfortableness to explore what you are feeling inside. Remember you are working toward the healing that comes from God, so you need to be open and honest and be willing to let His Holy Spirit "do some business" in your heart. This is your time, in the privacy of your own surroundings and between you and the Lord. Explore these deep areas of your life and let the Holy Spirit bring them to light. Take a moment to ask the Lord to open your heart and mind to the healing ahead.

Take a separate piece of paper and on each line, write one hurt that you have. You know. Go back as far as you can remember, beginning with your childhood years. Think about who hurt you. Was it your mom, your dad, your siblings, an extended family member, a friend, or a complete stranger? No need to write the person's name down, just the hurt. Was it the devastation of your parents' separation/divorce? Was it something that made you feel inadequate? Was it abuse of any kind? Was it a betrayal? If you were adopted or in foster homes, how does that truly make you feel? Where are the hurts? All of them!

Now, move forward to your teen years. Were there issues in your dating life? Were you raped? Did you have an abortion? Was it during *these* years that your family broke up? Were you bullied or made fun of? Step-parent issues? Did you get into drugs/alcohol/sexual promiscuity/crime? Write them down.

Early adulthood can be very challenging as we try to find out who we are away from our parents' beliefs and control. Many mistakes are made as we sort it all out. Who hurt you there? A boss, co-worker, stranger, a close relationship, sibling? Write them down. Did you end up being incarcerated? Did you feel alone and isolated? Abandoned and unloved? It is time to "get real".

You can put this list away until a future chapter when we will address these again. As you can see, if you were honest, hurt is a part of life and can chain us up in ways we haven't seen before. We can only push them aside for so long and then we see the effects they have on us as we live life. Healing is on the way for you, friend. These chains have held you long enough and Jesus is close by you, ready to help you break those chains.

You don't have to try and be strong, control your emotions and keep things in the past. It is time to be vulnerable, get the tissues out and lay it all out before the Lord. He hears you, He knows you, loves you and understands. He is ready to lift you up to freedom and joy. Ask Him to guide you through this chapter and show you how He can heal the emotions that may have been buried for a long time. If you are a guy, lay aside all the messages you have been taught about men not crying, never showing weakness or the importance of staying in control. You, no doubt, have every right to feel the anger, pain, betrayal, despair, and other emotions you feel today. Lay it out, guys and let God do His business in you so you can have more freedom, joy and true strength in your life.

Work it out in the Session 6 workbook pages as you discover more about your journey toward healing.

"The Lord is a Shelter for the oppressed, a Refuge in time of trouble. Those who know Your name trust in You, for You, O Lord, do not abandon those who search for You." Psalm 9:9-10 (NLT)

WEIGHT OF THE CHAIN

DEPRESSION

CHAPTER SEVEN
Weight Of The Chain
Facing Depression

We have all felt depression at one time or another in our lives. Sometimes it may be a day when we feel down and don't really want to leave the house. It just feels safer to stay in bed. Sometimes it can drop us into a deep valley and we *can't* leave the house for a long period of time. It can affect our jobs, relationships, health and virtually every area of our life.

Sometimes, you may look around and see happy families, celebrations, and others appear to enjoy life so much more than you do, while life seems to be passing you by. It can feel like you are stuck in a fog. Have you ever felt this way?

Depression is a large part of the Chain of Grief. It may last for just a short time or sometimes, it can continue for years. Depression is more than merely being sad. It is a lack of hope; hope that things will change. Hope that you will feel joy again. Hope that there are answers to the challenges you face. You will see the different levels of depression in the workbook and will be able to identify where you are on that scale. Depression can be anything from a lingering sadness to suicidal thoughts.

It can include sleepless nights or too much sleeping. Some people have an increased appetite and some can hardly eat. No matter what level of depression you might be in, if left unattended for a long period of time, it can be very harmful to your entire being. Depression can make you feel like giving up and is part of the Chain of Grief. You may come out of it for awhile, and then something will bring you right back down and life can become a rollercoaster.

How do you know you have depression and what are the first signs? Has anyone ever said, "You look down today?" or "What's wrong?" or "You don't seem like yourself." Do you find yourself staying alone and isolated more than you are out with people? Does the happiness of others annoy you or make you feel you are on the outside looking in?

This is a good time for you to evaluate yourself. Think about the following questions and answer them honestly.

Is your life fulfilling?
Do you enjoy getting outside?
Have you given up hobbies you once enjoyed?
Is the majority of your time spent alone?
Do you sense darkness surrounding you?

Have you seen how depression can just sort of sneak up and grab you and pull you down? It can begin with a hurtful situation like a broken relationship or loss of a job. It can increase by pulling away from others, not attending church or groups and maybe losing fellowship with God. It may be the situation you find yourself in right now and you are feeling buried by the hurt and emotion of it all.

At this time, if you are not feeling depressed as you go through this chapter, think of a time you may have experienced depression or felt hopeless. You may also know others who are struggling with depression and you have walked alongside of them.

When families break up because of divorce or death, children usually feel devastated and like they have no control over what just happened. Everything they know is being shattered; from holiday traditions, to family rituals, to the comfort of the house they had always known. Decisions are being made without their opinions or suggestions and many times, kids can just sort of "check out", isolate, and emotionally detach. They may spend most of their time in their rooms or "medicating" by playing endless hours of videogames or watching t.v., overeating, keeping overly busy, or spending time with their friends, just so they don't have to think about what is happening in their family. In essence, "If I ignore it, it might just go away". Don't we also do that as adults sometimes?

If your family broke up, you might have noticed that things you once were able to buy or restaurants you used to go to as a family were no longer happening. Waking up with both parents in the house or activities you once did as a family, were no longer in the picture. Maybe you couldn't buy new clothes anymore and had to purchase them at second hand stores or get hand me downs. Your life just seemed to get sadder and sadder every day until you just didn't care anymore. Was that your experience?

Stacy was a cute little blond girl who enjoyed playing Barbie dolls with her cousins, watching funny cartoons, playing soccer and just being a "normal" 7-year-old. People always said she was "such a happy little girl".

One day, Stacy heard her mommy and daddy arguing in their bedroom and inched closer to their door to hear what was going on. She heard her mommy crying and also heard the word "divorce". Stacy's best friend, Callie, had parents who got divorced and Stacy sure didn't want that to happen to her family! Callie wasn't as fun anymore after her parents split up. Callie was always going either to her dad's or mom's house and really didn't have a "home" anymore. She told Stacy that she was always saying goodbye and missing someone.

Well, Stacy's parents did end up separating and divorcing and Stacy wasn't as fun anymore either. Nothing seemed as amusing after that and Stacy began to withdraw. Her grades dropped and playing with Barbies didn't even make her happy. A cloud of depression began to form over her head. Her mom took her to a couple of different counselors in the next few years, but Stacy just couldn't seem to crawl out of this "hole".

During the next several years, as she became an adolescent, she began to sink lower and lower into depression. Nothing seemed to matter anymore. She found some friends who were feeling the same way she did and they began to hang out. They found that beer, wine and pot helped them to feel "better" and they spent most of their weekends "hanging out". They didn't care about school, getting a job or their futures. "Who cares anyway?"

Although not all children experience this scenario, many do. Many single parents are very attentive and put their children's needs and hurts before their own, no matter how depressed they are. On the other hand, many single parents can barely lift their heads and they live in a fog. In the "fog", parents may isolate themselves in their room while the kids stay outside or in other areas of the house. Many times, parents try to show others that they are fine, but when they get home, they fall onto their bed behind a closed door. Now, not only have the kids lost their parent who has walked away, they have also lost their other parent in the fog. What is a kid to do? Who will listen and can understand how *they* are feeling?

Depression can slightly affect you or it can debilitate you. If you have suffered or are suffering with depression for a long period of time and can't seem to make any headway, maybe it is time to talk to a professional about it. You might look into talking to a counselor, therapist, doctor, pastor or another trained professional. There can also be medical reasons for depression, so medication may be recommended.

Here are some steps to consider when working on the depression you may be experiencing and change your way of thinking:

STEP 1 - Realize and acknowledge you may be depressed. Get real about it and face it. You are not a loser or inept; you are depressed. You probably have very good reasons for being in this fog.

STEP 2 - Have a desire to get some answers and get better. Be willing to do what it takes. Talk to God about it and ask Him to give you answers, direction, and understanding.

STEP 3 - Get out there and don't isolate yourself. Be careful though, not to get so busy that you cover the depression and not deal with it.

STEP 4 - See a doctor and follow his/her instructions.

STEP 5 - See a pastor/counselor/therapist/chaplain, who uses God's Word to discuss recurring issues at length.

Imagine what it would be like to live life without the chains of depression, to see the positive things in life again, to be able to take full breaths each day and feel hope and joy once again. Isn't that what we all want?

Take some time to fill out the Session 7 workbook pages to explore depression, its causes, strategies to move out of it and what God's Word says about it. Life is too short to live in a fog or under the cloud of depression. Let's get to work and hopefully see the fog lifted!

"May our Lord Jesus Christ Himself and God our Father, Who loved us and gave us eternal comfort and a wonderful hope, comfort you and strengthen you in every good thing you do and say." II Thessalonians 2:16-17

GOD'S LINK TO YOU

"The Lord is the shelter for the oppressed, a refuge in time of trouble. Those who know Your name trust in You, for You, O Lord, have never abandoned anyone who searches for You."
(Psalm 9:9–10)

CHAPTER EIGHT
God's Link To You
Who God Is To You

This chapter begins the journey of healing and renewal as we look at God's Word and see who God is, what He thinks of us, and how we can receive His salvation and acceptance into His family.

It is our nature to let our circumstances or the opinions/expectations of others determine our self-worth, instead of basing it on who God says we are. Think about it...*we allow people who are as flawed and fickle as we are to determine our value.* How sad is that?! In the paragraphs below, try to identify the areas you struggled through as a kid and still today.

It begins when we are small children and the kids at school, even preschool, can accept us or make us feel like an outsider. Maybe another child calls us names, won't pick us for their team, or refuses to sit by us. We may cry out to our teachers and parents a lot, begin to act in anger or isolate because our value is already being tainted.

Middle school can escalate poor self-worth as all students try to fit in and figure out who they are. Not making the team again, being made fun of, not wearing the right clothes, or kids causing you to feel like you're on the outside looking in brings more isolation or acting out in negative ways.

Maybe you were a chubby kid or had bad teeth or perhaps you weren't very academic or athletic. Maybe your family could not afford the latest fashions or the coolest shoes. Kids can be very cruel to those who don't fit in and they can do that verbally, physically or by just plain ignoring them.

High school issues continue the pattern when boy-girl relationships become a factor. This society is filled with images and messages that teen sexual activity is a positive thing, when quite the opposite is true. Students go in and out of relationships at a rapid pace and with every breakup, a piece of an adolescent's self-worth and value is chipped away.

There are a lot more opportunities for kids to try to "fill the void" and they will gravitate to the people and places that make them feel accepted and valued, which could mean connecting with other hurting kids with negative behavior. Trying to cover the pain can cause children to isolate, self-medicate or sometimes work extra hard to be successful. They can even become popular, but inside, they may be crumbling and not feel they are worthy of anyone's love, time or even worthy to live.

Suicide in teens is a growing problem in our society today and it would be interesting to find out where the hurt began in each case. Most of the time, it comes from the devastation of their home life. Divorce, abuse, parents remarrying, daily chaos, consuming anger and rage in the house, and on and on..... We cannot be surprised that these kids find no other way to escape the pain than to check out of life altogether while the parents ask "why?"

If there are problems with relationships at home, they can isolate even more. Many of these children can feel like they will never be or do things well enough to please their parents, so they often stop trying. They feel like they are nothing but an inconvenience to their parents, who are dealing with their own issues. Children don't really know where they belong and where their identity lies so they reach for anything or anyone to fill the void to give them a sense of belonging. Do you see how a pattern can be continued throughout a child's life and into adulthood?

Now, let's add another element to the scenario. A child's father may have left the home and has little communication with his son or daughter. To the child, they feel abandoned and may be thinking, "Even my own father didn't love me enough to stay!" This is especially true for little girls, whose first "love" relationship is with her daddy. If her father has walked out of her life, she will usually try for the rest of her days to "fill that void" searching for relationships with guys that she so desperately needs. She may become promiscuous, dress more provocatively, hang out and cling to older men, or find she just cannot live without a relationship with a guy. She needs to feel valuable and desirable and will do almost anything to fill that emptiness in her heart. Another reaction may be that she becomes very bitter about guys and will never know the joy of having a healthy relationship. The issues of trust, abandonment, and betrayal come to the forefront of a girl's existence as she grows into an adult.

How different her life could have been if she had a loving and healthy relationship with her daddy, felt protected by him, was provided for and truly felt valued by her own father. There are millions of children living without a father in the home in America today. What a shame for an entire generation!

What a difference it would make to these same children if they realized that God made them, says they are beautiful in His sight, gives them special gifts and talents, plus loves and accepts them just the way they are!

This chapter will explore your thoughts and beliefs about God. Your birth family may have not had a strong faith background. You may not have gone to church as a child, or only went on holidays or out of obligation. On the other hand, your family may have truly plugged into a strong and vibrant congregation. Whatever the case, this chapter will allow you to see where you came from as far as faith is concerned.

The church is filled with imperfect people just like you and me, who have daily struggles no matter how nice they look as they walk into the church building on Sundays. They struggle with their faith and seek healing for hurts in their lives too. Many times, people outside of the church just say, "All Christians are just hypocrites who are weak and need to lean on something or Someone." "They just want our money and are not afraid to ask for it." "Christians are very judgmental, as far as I am concerned." "I don't want to be part of that." "I can do life by myself."

Believe me, I have heard it all. Sometimes we Christians are some or all of those things for sure. We don't seem to see the perception that unbelievers have of us or maybe we don't even care. We should. If we are going to look at human beings, in or out of the church, we will always be able to see flaws and inconsistencies. That is part of being a human being. Only God is the perfect One.

When we seek forgiveness from the Lord God of the universe, He gives it, which does not mean we can do anything we want and then just run to Him to get off the hook. He accepts human beings for exactly who we are and sees the potential of who we can become. His love and acceptance has no limits. Wow! That is certainly different from the type of love we human beings have for one another, isn't it?

What do you believe in? Do you have those beliefs because your parents did or have you taken them as your own? Do you believe the Bible is the Word of God? What has God done for you or have you noticed? Who is God to you?

These are questions we all wrestle with at some time in our lives. We may wrestle with them throughout our life, depending upon what's going on. Maybe you gave your heart and life to Jesus when you were a child in Sunday School, or maybe you made a commitment to Him when you were a teen at summer camp or a youth event. Maybe He found you when you were homeless or in prison. You may have accepted Christ as an adult – or maybe you have never put your faith in Him.

Whatever the case, He created you, He sees you, He knows you, He has never taken His eye off of you and He wants to have a loving relationship with you. God has a purpose for you and this purpose remains the same no matter how your circumstances change throughout your life.

He didn't cause the problems you have had in your life, but He was always nearby to help you through them if you were to ask Him. He could have prevented those challenges, yes, but for some reason He did not. We will talk about some good things that may have come from your past struggles in a later session.

This Father will not walk away, hurt us, yell at us, abuse us, ignore us or treat us like we are nothing. *This* Father does not keep records of all our mistakes and bad decisions. *This* Father loves us for exactly who we are. We don't need be perfect to come to Him.

If you could ask God one question, what would it be? If you could spend some time with Him discussing things that concern you, what would you say? What do you think He would say to you?

Please take some paper and write a long letter to God right now. Take your time to think about what you want to ask or say. If you are mad at Him, tell Him. If you question why He allowed things to happen in your life, ask Him. If you don't believe in Him or don't know if you do, tell Him that and ask Him to reveal Himself to you. If you just want to thank Him for things, do that. He hears you and He knows everything about you, big or small. He knows your past and He certainly knows your future. He knew you would be sitting here right now, reading this chapter. He knows you are seeking healing for all that has hurt you. He is here.

Praying is just talking to the Father God, sharing your true feelings and thoughts, seeking Him for answers and praising Him for who He is. Let Him hear your heart and what lies deep within you.

Are you mad that He didn't prevent your abuse, losses, painful relationships, loss of finances, deaths of loved ones, etc? Do you question His very existence? Maybe you have given your life to Him and are trying to live a life He would want you to, but have questions of how to do that. Maybe you are seeking His will for your life in some decisions you have to make. Maybe you are filled with shame about your past. Maybe you are scared for things that your kids are doing that could ruin their lives, or there are uncertain health issues that have come up for you or someone you love. Maybe you are in a situation that seems impossible and the hurt overwhelms you. Write it in your letter to Him.

Don't forget to thank Him for hearing you and loving you just for who you are today. He hears every word, but more importantly, He hears your heart. He wants you to be real with Him and begin a dialogue. A dialogue, however, includes talking *and* listening, so as you communicate with Him, He will communicate with you. Listen to what He brings to your mind. He's there. Shhhhhh.

"Do not be anxious about anything, but in everything, by prayer and petition, with thanksgiving, present your requests to God, and the peace of God, which transcends all understanding will guard your hearts and your minds in Christ Jesus." Philippians 4:6,7

"For I know the plans I have for you," declares the Lord, "plans to prosper you and not to harm you. Plans to give you hope and a future. Then you will call on Me and come and pray to Me and I will listen to you. You will seek Me and find Me when you seek Me with all your heart." Jeremiah 29:11-13

Take your time as you explore your faith in the workbook pages of Chapter 8. He will meet you there if you ask Him to.

LETTING GO OF THE CHAIN

FORGIVENESS

CHAPTER NINE
Letting Go Of The Chain
Receiving And Giving Forgiveness

Do you remember your mom demanding that you say, "I'm sorry" to people when you were a kid? You usually said it even if you didn't mean it, right? "I'm SORRY", you would say with your arms folded and your bottom lip stuck out.

Is it easy for you to forgive people who have offended you? Is it easy for you to ask for forgiveness from others? The subject of forgiveness is difficult and has many layers, but extraordinarily important to the process of healing.

We have all been hurt and let down throughout our lives. Why is it so hard to forgive some people and easier to forgive others? Maybe it depends on the level of pain they caused us. Hurts like betrayal, abandonment or abuse of any kind can be harder to forgive than a lie, miscommunication, embarrassment, etc. Maybe it depends how close we are to them, so the offense hits deeper. Maybe we weren't shown forgiveness, so we don't have a forgiving heart either.

Sometimes the hurt is too great, and we continue to live in the darkness of bitterness and unforgiveness. Living with unforgiveness can be like cancer on our heart and affect layers upon layers in our life. Bitterness is kind of like another cover emotion, which hides issues such as hurt, fear, embarrassment, betrayal, abandonment, etc. If we "hang our hat" on bitterness and unforgiveness, then we may never really look at and deal with the issues under it, which keep us from being free. More chains.

No matter what the offense was, it is important to take steps toward forgiveness. Forgiving someone doesn't take *them* off the hook as much as it takes *you* off the hook. It doesn't mean you necessarily forget the offense either. Some things are just too painful to forget, right? It means you say, "I RELEASE YOU FROM THE PAIN YOU CAUSED ME; IT WILL HAVE NO POWER OVER ME ANYMORE!"

You see, when you remain in unforgiveness and anger, you are still giving the person who offended you power over you on some deep levels. You are allowing them to take your joy, freedom, and peace of mind. You are allowing them to make you feel less than your best. You are allowing them to make you keep score as well as the desire to "settle the score", which God says is His to settle.

"Do not seek revenge or bear a grudge against one of your people, but love your neighbor as yourself." Leviticus 19:18

"Do not take revenge, my friends, but leave room for God's wrath, for it is written: 'It is mine to avenge; I will repay,' says the Lord." Romans 12:19

The last passage even goes on to say, *"If your enemy is hungry, feed him; if he is thirsty, give him something to drink. In doing this, you will heap burning coals on his head. Do not be overcome by evil, but overcome evil with good."* Can you see yourself doing that?! Being at least civil to your ex-spouse, your parents, your abuser, that old relationship, someone at work, etc. is what He is asking of us. Another step of submission to the Lord God that isn't easy, but right.

Carolyn was 18 when she met who she thought was the love of her life and her soul mate. Jason was the captain of the basketball and football team at her high school. Everyone cheered for him and it made her feel so proud to be his girlfriend. They talked of marrying someday after college and starting a future together. Everything seemed right on track until one day, four years later, she found out that he was seeing another girl who he worked with and they were serious. When she

Chained No More

confronted him, he told Carolyn that he was no longer in love with her and he wanted to break up immediately. She later found out that Jason's new love was pregnant and they were getting married.

Carolyn was shattered and withdrew for many months. It seemed like her life was over and there was nothing to live for. Her future had been planned and now nothing fit. "There is no way I could *ever* forgive Jason for this and I *won't*", she would fiercely yell. "He doesn't deserve my forgiveness. This is too big and he has ruined my life. I'll bet you that even God won't forgive him for what he did to me!"

Have you ever been as angry as Carolyn and felt that way? Maybe you try to think of ways to get back at someone for what they did to you. Maybe you are one who is really good at playing the martyr and wanting to make sure everyone knows you were wronged so they will feel sorry for you. Maybe you shrink back and your heart hardens little by little. Do you see the power that person has over you? They may have wronged you, but *you* are letting them ruin your life. You are letting them define you. *You.* More chains.

Forgiveness, many times, needs to happen for something you have lost, maybe wrong decisions by people you love, perhaps from your own mistakes or for just the way things eventually turned out.

Often we are good at pinning all the anger and unforgiveness on the other person and forget that we are only responsible for our own actions, words and feelings. *We* let them keep us in the chains of unforgiveness. *We* let them steal our joy. *We* let them cover peace in our lives. Does this hit home for you today? Think for a moment of people or situations who keep you bound in unforgiveness and pain. Now, do those memories cause you to feel tension or get emotional, whether it be anger or sadness or another emotion? If they do, they still have power over you.

Let's take a right turn now and look at Jesus and all those who hated Him, spit on Him, ridiculed Him, and hurt Him in almost every possible way. Why did He allow that to happen when He could have taken a breath and obliterated all of them in an instant? Why did He allow Himself to be dragged through the streets in front of thousands and then be placed on a huge wooden cross with his hands and feet nailed to that cross with spikes? After being raised up so all could see, how could He say, "Father, forgive them"? Try to picture this scene in your mind, if you can.

Why did He do that? Because that is what His Heavenly Father asked of Him and because He knew He was enduring all of this to make payment for the sins of all of us throughout time. Humanly speaking, it is beyond my comprehension why someone would do that for me or anyone else. This is not some gory story; it is *truth* and it is for you right here and right now.

Jesus did that for *you.* He wants to forgive *you* for every sin *you* have ever committed or will commit. All He asks of you is for you to ask Him for forgiveness from those sins and believe in Who He is and what He did. He wants to wipe the slate clean and become the Lover of your soul. He wants to surround you and fill you with His Spirit this very moment. He made you, loves you, and wants to accept you as one of His very own children. If you are ready to let Him become the Savior of your heart and soul, please go to the workbook and read "God's Truths On Forgiveness" in Chapter 9 and then turn the page to the "Sinner's Prayer".

If you said that prayer, you are now a child of God and your adventure has just begun. Oh, you'll still have problems and challenges in life, but now you have a Heavenly Father who can guide you, encourage you through His Word and share sweet fellowship with you. Hallelujah!

At the bottom of the "Sinner's Prayer" page, you will find a list of things that can help you become stronger and grow as a Christian. Also, they will enable you to experience His joy and peace in your life. Sound good?

The beauty of this is that once you experience God's unconditional forgiveness, you can move forward and begin to forgive those who have hurt you. You can be free of those chains of unforgiveness and they won't have power over you anymore!

Do you remember the hurts you wrote out in Chapter 6? Please look at that list of hurts. Forgiving is one of the hardest things you may ever have to do, but the benefits are enormous and life changing. Isn't that one of the reasons you are going through "Chained No More"?

Forgiveness is directly referenced 125 times in the Bible, so obviously, it is important to God for His children. Like my friend, Krista Smith says, in her book, "The Big D...Divorce Thru the Eyes of a Teen"... "Forgiveness is a promise. Forgiveness is a pledge. Forgiveness is a statement of undeserved, unearned, love that says, no matter what you've done, there is no desire for paybacks or punishment. This is not something we can do on our own. It is only through the grace that God demonstrates to us that gives us the strength to extend the gift of forgiveness to others." So, the question remains...why is it so important to forgive?

- Because Jesus forgave us (Ephesians 4:32 Luke 23:34)
- Because it frees us from bitterness (Hebrews 12:14-15)
- Because it demonstrates Christ's character (Colossians 3:12-13)
- Because it will deliver us from Satan's traps (II Corinthians 2:9-11)
- Because it delivers us from the discipline from God (Luke 6:35-37a)
- Because if we expect to be forgiven, we ourselves need to forgive (James 2:13)

God continues to forgive us for our wrongs, so as we have been forgiven, we can extend forgiveness to others who have hurt us. Go to the Chapter 9 workbook page with the cross on it. Place it in front of you for this life changing activity. Now, find the list of hurts you wrote in Chapter 6.....

Start at the top of the list. With each hurt, think about who caused that hurt, what it felt like and how has affected you. Repeat this phrase out loud, "I RELEASE YOU FROM THE PAIN YOU CAUSED ME. IT WILL HAVE NO POWER OVER ME...ANYMORE!" If you can honestly release that person who caused the pain, cross off that hurt and write it on the cross. Continue through the list and repeat. If you just cannot forgive someone yet, do not cross the hurt off the list nor write it on the cross. Be real and honest. This is between you and the Lord God. Fill the cross up with forgiven hurts and if you run out of room, just write one forgiven hurt on top of another. Know that His heart and the cross are big enough to handle them all. Forgive. Forgive. Forgive.

This important exercise can be very emotional, but can be very freeing indeed. Those chains have been broken, but what do you do now? In the next chapter, you will learn the "Click Points" tool that you will be able to use to move forward. These same people who have hurt you can come back into your life and try to hurt you again. Remember that you have placed your hurts at the cross. You can't really help what another person does, but you sure can keep them from having that power over you again.

Please go to the workbook pages for Chapter 9 now and work through this transforming chapter on forgiveness after praying that the Holy Spirit will open your eyes and heart and free you from these chains.

"Bear with each other and forgive whatever grievances you may have against one another. Forgive as the Lord forgave you." Colossians 3:13

Chapter Ten

BREAKING THE CHAIN

If you hold to My teaching, you are really My disciples.
Then you will know the truth and the truth will set you free!
(John 8:31–32)

SCENARIO #2 – You have been reminded of a past mistake or behavior you made that caused great hurt to someone. It brings you back to feelings of guilt and maybe even shame. You begin to get depressed and start "beating yourself up" again. That happened so long ago! Why does it still take hold of you?

STOP! *Click Point.* Apologies were said, the relationship was restored. Everyone supposedly moved on, right? The Lord God forgave you and the offended person forgave you. Why can't you forgive yourself and truly move on too? Why do you hold on?

Realize that the enemy is fighting for your mind, your heart and your freedom. That is his job and his goal is to keep you in this faulty and hurtful mindset. He knows that if he wins this battle, he will keep you from having victory over it and your faith will weaken. Say, "In the name of Jesus, I will *not* let the enemy win this battle again. It is under the blood, forgiven and forgotten by God Himself. I will *not* allow the enemy to keep me chained with this and I *will* step over him now!" Speak it out loud and clear!

In other words, as soon as you recognize these battles, it is important for you to *immediately* remove and replace faulty thinking the enemy throws at you with the truth of the Word of God and with His strength and light.

"Click Points" are effective tools to use every single time you find yourself caught up in faulty thinking or negative patterns. The sooner you recognize these challenges, the better, as you continue to walk toward freedom from the chains of your past. With every victory, you will be able to get stronger, be more positive and live life more joyfully. The enemy will not have a hold and you can move forward and live free.

In this chapter, we want to explore who you *really* are. You are unique! You have gifts, talents, a specific temperament and spiritual gifts that you could use to help others and glorify God. Wouldn't it be amazing to be able to be free to be the *real* you?

The enemy, Satan, doesn't want us to find our identity in who God says we are. He wants us to try and do everything on our own, to fail at anything positive, live in darkness and not serve God in any way. He wants us to be angry and bitter, and he influences that part of us constantly. That is his self-proclaimed purpose and goal: to keep us far from God and any relationship with Him. What he keeps forgetting, however, is that God is bigger than he is and because God loves us, He wants a loving relationship with us and will win the battle for our heart if we will let Him.

The enemy may have covered you in chains and with every link that is broken, he loses one more hold on you. On the workbook page "Identity Theft…Who Am I *Really*" in the workbook pages of this chapter, you will see who God meant you to be. It may be something you have never known or maybe you have heard these truths before but have forgotten them. When you go over this page, please say the verses out loud with strength and conviction because you are speaking truth with every word. Let these messages from God's Word penetrate your heart and spirit while coming out of your mouth.

Think of this chapter as a wrapped gift you are going to be opening. Inside this magnificent present, you will find the beautiful truths of who you are without all the garbage that came before, without all the chains you have been dragging through your life. This is the truth about you, friend. Leave all the negative messages you have heard and lived with for so many years and keep them outside of this present. There is no place for them here. You are who God says you are; nothing more and nothing less.

"The Lord is faithful to all His promises and loving toward all He has made. The Lord upholds all those who fall and lifts up all who are bowed down. The Lord is near to all who call on Him, to all who call on Him in truth; He fulfills the desires of those who fear Him; He hears their cry and saves them." Psalm 145:13b-14, 18,19

Now, let's go to the Session 10 workbook pages and open the gift of joy, acceptance, grace and love. Meet the *real* you!

Chapter Eleven

LOVE LINKS
LOVE & RELATIONSHIPS

LOVE...bears all things, believes all things, hopes all things, endures all things. Love NEVER fails.
1 Corinthians 1:13

CHAPTER ELEVEN
Love Links
Love And Relationships

Ahhh....the subject of love. In this chapter, you will be exploring your thoughts and attitudes about a love relationship, learn about trust and respect in a healthy marriage, reflecting on your family patterns and beliefs about vows and commitment, learning healthier ways to deal with conflict and confrontations and exploring what God's Word says about love. "Wait a minute! This is just overload! I have failed at relationships so many times. They just don't work out for me. I have just about given up any hope!" Is that what you are saying right now?

Do you believe it is possible for you to have a lifelong marriage without divorce? Why or why not? Just to remind you, one of the most important things to believe is that just because your parents separated/divorced, it doesn't mean that you are predestined to the same failure. Maybe you are or have been in a loving, vibrant and successful marriage or maybe you have already been unsuccessful at relationships or marriage. Perhaps that is a big reason you are seeking healing now, to find out why you can't seem to have healthy relationships and to possibly learn how.

Your ideas about love and marriage may have been influenced mostly by your parents' relationship. You have probably seen good times and you may have also seen the failure of their marriage. Maybe the vast amount of marriages you know have been failures and you are now assuming that it isn't possible for you to have a long-term healthy marriage in the world today either. Maybe your parents never married, so you have barely any experience with marriage at all.

This may have left you with a fear of commitment or any hope that your marriage could be successful. You may find it difficult to trust or are afraid your spouse will abandon you, so why set yourself up for more hurt and failure? Possibly all you remember about your parents is them arguing or fighting and you sure don't want to repeat that pattern in *your* life. Sound familiar?

Let's get down to basics and ask the question again. Do you believe it is possible for you to have a lifelong marriage without divorce? Why or why not? Think about that for a minute or two. (Your own history, past examples of divorce, parents' divorce or separation, statistics, media that glamorizes it, etc.)

God invented love and marriage. The love He wanted for His children to enjoy is unconditional love, a love that is not selfish, competitive, hurtful, jealous, controlling or arrogant.

"Love is *patient*, love is *kind*, and is *not jealous*; love does *not brag*, and is *not arrogant*, does not act unbecomingly; it does *not seek its own*, is *not provoked*, does *not take into account a wrong suffered*, does *not rejoice in unrighteousness*, but rejoices with the truth. Love *bears* all things, *believes* all things, *hopes* all things, *endures* all things. *Love never fails!*" I Corinthians 13:4-8a

This is the love that the Lord had in mind when He invented love and marriage. He didn't invent the flawed and failed love and marriage that so many of us have experienced. What happened and how did we stray so far from God's ideal for what should be a source of joy and contentment in our lives?

We have become a self-centered society of wanting what we want when we want it and how we want it. We deserve this and we don't deserve that. If we don't get what we want or need, then we are going to move on. We will leave before we are left. We allow ourselves to be tempted right into an extramarital affair instead of turning toward our spouse and working on the issues together. Sometimes we can get so involved in outside interests that we leave our husband/wife in the dust and then are surprised when they walk away.

Many times, we look toward the place where we get the most encouragement or where we excel. Because things are not ideal at home, we may look away from our spouse/family and toward our job or where we feel the best about ourselves. That is the easy way out, because we are not willing to put in the work to improve what is happening in our personal relationships.

If you have been divorced, think back on the day you got married and all that your wedding experience may have been like. The flowers, woman in the pretty dress, man in the handsome suit, love in the air, pretty music, the vows, the rings, commitment and the fun and joy of the reception. Maybe this description does not match with your experience at all. Your wedding may have been an afternoon at the justice of the peace, in someone's backyard, or in a little chapel in Vegas. Maybe you didn't marry for love at all, but to get out of your parents' house, or you were forced to marry because of a pregnancy or by a controlling person in your life. Maybe you were just too young to know better and it sounded like the exciting thing to do. Maybe it was all a big mistake. Maybe you have never been married and just lived with someone, but you have seen both successful and unsuccessful marriages in friends and family.

Sometimes, even the wedding and the months leading up to the wedding had warning signs that this wasn't the best idea. Maybe the arguments, control issues and family drama reared their ugly heads, but you ignored them and chalked them up to the stress of the event. Possibly you felt stuck because money had been spent, reservations made or it was too embarrassing to cancel the event. Were you being set up for failure even then?

If you have been married more than once, there are other issues to explore. If we have not resolved them or healed from them, we can take our baggage from one relationship to another (baggage such as an unfaithful spouse, financial control, abuse of any kind, abandonment, betrayal, etc.). We come into the next relationship with deep wounds and many times the new relationship pays for the relationships we had before. This doesn't set anyone or any relationship up for success. This is one of the primary goals of "Chained No More"...to help you heal from wounds in the past so you can move forward toward a much healthier future and enjoy positive and successful relationships of all kinds.

There are tools and lessons to be learned in this session to help set you up for success in marriage; a marriage based on God's principles of love and marriage. These concepts are the ideal and something for us to all shoot for. Fight for your marriage, your vows and commitment and for His design in marriage. Society and our American media stand for the opposite, but God's Word is truth.

"The fruit of the Spirit is love, joy, peace, patience, kindness, goodness, faithfulness, gentleness and self-control". (Galatians 5:22,23) Were these elements in each of your past relationships? How about in your parents' marriage? Which ones were missing? Now, a marriage based on these principles in Galatians will be successful and can last a lifetime!

Steve and Brittani were in the final stages of preparing for their June wedding. The venue and the priest had been reserved and the cake, music, and decorations were taken care of. They planned for about 150 people to attend this occasion.

This was the second marriage for Brittani and the third one for Steve and they wanted this time to be different. They had both read books about having a successful stepfamily, had gone to some counseling at their church and were ready to tackle the challenges and enjoyed the thought of having a big happy family. Between the two of them, they had four children and they knew it would take a lot of effort. They believed they would do fine because of their strong love for each other.

A month before the big day, the tension of the wedding reared its ugly head and the couple had a sizeable argument. Steve had gone out of town on business and forgot to call Brittani that night. She left several messages and each one sounded more tense than the last. Brittani started to remember when her ex-husband, Greg began to do this, and then she found out he was involved in an affair, which shattered their marriage. Oh, no, not again! She began to imagine all kinds of scenarios and became convinced that Steve was cheating on her too!

The next morning, Steve called to apologize for forgetting to call her and Brittani verbally attacked him through her tears. The truth was that Steve's company meeting ran until late into the night and he was so tired, that he fell asleep on the hotel bed in his clothes. He forgot to even turn his phone on when he got back to the room.

After listening to Brittani's hurt for a few minutes, Steve stopped her by saying, "Honey, I am so sorry that I hurt you so much. Please forgive me. Brittani, I am not Greg; I am Steve." Do you see how Brittani had transferred the hurt she suffered with Greg to the man she was marrying in a month?

This couple did get married in June, brought their families together and even though they had similar conflicts for a while, they built strong trust in each other over time and enjoyed a good marriage.

Each person comes into a new relationship having his or her own experiences and expectations whether they are good or unhealthy. Many times, couples don't know enough about each other's journey up to that point and so they don't have a chance to work through things and see how they are going to build a healthy relationship. It is *highly* recommended that both you and your partner get strong Christian counseling to work through issues and figure out how you are going to bring two lives together in a healthy way so your future as a couple can be strong, vibrant and long lasting. If your partner does not agree to go to pre-marital counseling, please take a step back and see why they don't feel a relationship with you is worth a few hours of preventative action toward a healthy marriage. It is worth the pause.

Every marriage is worth taking valuable time to explore each other's past and the issues rooted there. Examine your spiritual beliefs and practices to see if you are unified and compatible in that vital area of your relationship. Compare your emotional strengths and weaknesses. How do each of you handle conflicts and confrontations? Sexual issues? Financial pressures? What are your values in life? Who have been your role models of marriage and/or commitments which might positively or negatively affect your relationship with each other?

You should feel the best about yourself at home, but that may become impossible if your partner is controlling, isolating, or so independent that you come second to their desires and interests. Another big issue in couples is when they let other family members become too involved. Each family member have their own issues and loyalties and they can cause much more tension and division in the relationship you are involved in. It is essential to set up clear boundaries and be consistent in using them.

If each of you takes your vows with the underlying belief, that if it doesn't work there is always a way out, you will not be able to make a full commitment to the relationship. The threat of separation/divorce may become a part of what you say in an argument and it chips away at your commitment.

It is important to remember that you cannot change someone else, only yourself. Many people go into a marriage thinking if there is a trait they don't like in the other person, they can change him/her. They find out later the "trait" never does go away and may even escalate after they sign the marriage certificate. Only God can change a life and only if we allow Him to.

Marriage, in God's perfect design, was meant to be "until death do us part". When you say those vows, you are saying them to God first and your spouse secondly. It is something to be sure of, and then completely commit to.

Take your time, observe, question, listen to your heart and pray that God will lead you into a strong, loving, encouraging and joyful marriage. It is well worth your time and your devotion if it is God's plan for you.

You may have been married for years and your marriage has become complacent and kind of status quo. There is a lot of water under the bridge that may have left both of you separately living in the same house with only a platonic relationship. When is the last time you held your spouse and told him/her you really loved them and meant it? Do your actions show your love or is your spouse left guessing? When is the last time you told your spouse what you appreciate or respect them for? Are there underlying issues that have never been resolved? Is your marriage what the Lord designed it to be or do you care about that? How would you like your relationship to look and what are you willing to do about it? It is amazing how our relationships change when we change. This chapter will help you explore the issues of love, trust and respect. Are you ready for that and do you have an open heart and mind for it?

Now, what happens when trust has been broken, and there is no trust or respect? What if there is betrayal or abandonment? What do you do if your spouse has walked away from God and is out of fellowship with Him? How do you develop good communication skills with needed confrontation? How long will you go with hidden feelings, stuffing them inside and trying to just survive? Is that what you are doing now? Have you lost your self-respect? What kind of example are your kids seeing about how spouses should treat each other? When is enough *enough*? What boundaries do you need to set up so your home is one of peace, love, and respect? Anything less is not God's best for you or your family. The most difficult question is: When is it time to "let go"? In this session, you will be able to explore confrontation skills to help, but please don't ignore the need for professional and/or pastoral help, especially if there is ongoing abuse.

Go to session 11 workbook pages to get started. Please take your time as you explore this important subject. Take the time to sit and meditate on the principles and tools. They are here for you to take them all in, apply them and walk in them. This is not a fast track for you to just jump into a relationship. It takes time to work through all of this and besides; it isn't just about you, is it? There is another person involved and may include children. You want your family to be healthy, so you and your spouse can be set up for relationship success, right? Let's get started!

MAKING A NEW CHAIN

(Part One)

...ONE LINK AT A TIME

CHAPTER TWELVE
Making A New Chain (Part One)
Changing Old Patterns

This chapter is all about examining your thoughts and behavior patterns and how they affect your life. It will also help you look at how you would like your life to be different, as well as look at your hopes and dreams. Do you *have* hopes and dreams? Do you remember having them as a kid?

Maybe you had dreams of being a happy, carefree kid who played sports, sang, enjoyed going to the movies or picnics, or camping as one happy family. Maybe you had hopes of playing baseball with your dad and growing up to be just like him; a hero in your mind. Maybe you had dreams of being married with the traditional white picket fence with 2.5 children. Maybe you had dreams of being a fireman, a movie star, a teacher or an artist. What happened? Did your dreams come true?

On the other hand, maybe you never had any dreams because you were just trying to survive day to day in your environment. Maybe your fear for your safety clouded your mind on a daily basis. You may have decided that all kids must live this way. Dreams? What dreams?

Kids are born into their parents' environment and sometimes have to grow up very fast for a variety of reasons. There may have been abuse, a parent with addictions, neglect, or abandonment. You may have tried to live out your parents' hopes for you, or had too many responsibilities or activities. Maybe your parents didn't know how to just let you be a kid of innocence, hopes and dreams. What happened to that little boy/girl you were meant to be?

Many times, as adults, living with shattered hopes and dreams, we get so caught up in life that we don't allow ourselves to envision what our future could look like. In doing that, we may miss out on what God has planned for us. This session can be very enlightening and exciting, as you look forward with hope and healing. You are a new person with broken chains of your past now and can explore the "new you" and what the future could hold.

You will examine your old patterns of thoughts and behavior, think about how you were and what you want to become, reflect on the influences you have in your life and how they may be affecting you. Then you can allow yourself to look at your dreams for the future and find a way to achieve them.

This is another chapter of looking forward instead of just looking back. It is, in essence, "looking out of the windshield instead of the rearview mirror". Think about that for a moment. If you were driving a car and all you did was look out the rearview mirror, you could bump into things, run off the road or could be fatally injured. If you just looked out of the windshield and never checked your rearview mirror, you might be hit from behind and not see a potential danger approaching.

The same thing goes for our lives. If we just look at our past and live in its issues, we cannot move forward in safety and strength. If we only look forward, but not remember what was before, we could fall back into the same traps and patterns we were in. The past needs to be dealt with, but not completely forgotten. It is part of who we are, but it doesn't have to have power over us or define us as we "drive away from it". Does that make sense?

No matter how old we are, there is always room for change and improvement. This doesn't mean we can never be content, but it does mean that we should continually strive to become more like Christ, living life to the fullest, using the gifts and talents He has given to us for His glory.

We need to stop comparing ourselves to other flawed human beings, whether it is how we look, how much we have materially, where we fit in and *if* we fit in. The question is: "Are we pleasing to the Lord and living up to *His* plan for us"? Now, *that* is the best life we could ever live!

Please go find a handheld mirror, if you have one. If you don't, just go to a mirror and take this book with you. Look at your reflection for a moment.

What do you see when you look in the mirror? Do you see a perfect face, someone with a perfect body? Is it even difficult to look at yourself in the mirror? Do you see someone who has it all together, or do you see someone who is flawed? Do you see deep sadness, great joy or somewhere in between? Do you see years of guilt and shame clouding your reflection? Do you see someone who has a hurting heart, or someone who has received healing from the Lord Jesus?

Do you see only what a human can see or who God says you are? Do you see years of insecurity or a growing faith and confidence in your standing with Him? Take some time to look in the mirror. Look deep and get real. *That* is the face that Jesus loves. *That* is the person who Jesus forgives, accepts and will never walk away from. *That* is the person who is valued by the Lord God.

Gayle was a beautiful, tall African-American woman who had spent much of her life trying to impress people with her looks, her clothes and her intelligence. It was vitally important for her to have people admire her and think she could do no wrong. She was a perfectionist in almost all she did. She was a cheerleader, president of many clubs in high school and was crowned homecoming queen. She was on the honor role every year and headed to college with a full academic scholarship. She wanted to prove to the world that an African-American woman could be successful and be respected. Life was good and just the way she liked it.

Underneath this perfection-driven woman was a hurting child of divorce. She felt the divorce was largely her fault and tried to be perfect so her parents might get back together. She never felt she was good enough or would ever meet her parents' expectations, but she just kept trying. Maybe they would tell her she was loved if she did all the right things. Every time she would bring her report cards home when she was a kid, she waited for a compliment, an encouraging word or even an acknowledgement that she did well. Never came. They only saw where she fell short. She just kept trying. She found her worth in those who lived outside of her own home.

When she got into college, she had visions continuing her successes of being popular, getting involved in many things, making lots of friends and having relationships with gorgeous athletic guys. It didn't turn out that way.

Gayle had a roommate who, from day one, did not like her and Gayle just *knew* Ann was jealous of Gayle's beauty and all of her fine clothes. Every day was filled with tension and bad vibes so Gayle began to look for other people to hang out with. There were the older students who were going back to college, the athletes, cheerleaders, science geeks, and the partiers whose parents just wanted them to "live the experience of college life". Where did she fit in now? She felt invisible and was miserable. She couldn't seem to impress anyone!

One day, she noticed a good looking guy in the café who kept glancing at her over his laptop. He looked like one of the basketball players for the school. His dark skin and big white smile interested her. She was having some issues with her computer, so decided to go meet him and strike up a conversation. They talked for a while and exchanged phone numbers. That afternoon began a long story of love and hate, compliments and putdowns, control and out of control issues and left Gayle feeling like a needy failure, a shadow of who she was before. For many years to come, she would spend her time looking for love, acceptance and value. Why?

Because she let others, who were as flawed as she was, determine her self-worth. She allowed them to make her feel devalued, "less than", ugly at times and not worth anyone's time or attention. It was crushing and kept her from growing and developing into the woman she was meant to be or strived to be. No matter how many fashion magazines she read or which diets she tried, she never felt she could measure up to those around her; or, at least, that is what she thought. She just kept trying to get the approval of others for her value. What a futile way to live!

Do you see how looking through the rearview mirror can keep you from looking through the windshield and moving forward? It can happen to anyone, but there is always hope with healing in Jesus Christ. Looking forward will make you stronger by enabling you to take essential steps. This will restore your confidence and result in a more joyful, healthier life for you.

This is *your* life and you have the opportunity now to move forward in strength and experience joy, free from the chains you have been dragging through life. This is the new *you*!

"Do not conform any longer to the pattern of this world, but be transformed by the renewing of your mind. Then you will be able to test and approve what God's will is – His good, pleasing and perfect will." Romans 12:2

Please turn to the Chapter 12 workbook pages and let's get started! You've got some growing to do!

MAKING A NEW CHAIN
(Part Two)

...ONE LINK AT A TIME

CHAPTER THIRTEEN
Making A New Chain (Part Two)
Developing New Patterns

How comfortable are you with changes in your life? Is it difficult for you to adjust to change or do you embrace change and make the necessary adjustments? Changes such as a new responsibility at work or a change of hairstyle can be easily accepted while changes like moving to a new house, changing jobs or going through a divorce can completely throw you.

Life changes can feel like a train whizzing by while you stand beside the track. It can almost knock you over and make you unsteady for a long period of time. Sometimes, however, you barely notice changes at all.

Change can be difficult especially if we have had the same patterns and habits for a long time. It takes one step at a time, making strong efforts to change. It can be freeing and exciting when we finally realize we did it!

Some changes are easier to make than others. Some habits take longer to break than others. The first step to change is identifying a goal of change, determining the steps and taking those steps one at a time with strong resolve and purpose.

You may find yourself in a dark place at the present time and you see no way out. Maybe there is nothing you can do to change your circumstances, but God can help you change your perspective and make the most of where you are. Seem impossible? The truth is: *Nothing* is impossible with God and His plan. God's desire for those He loves is for you to be the best you can be and to accomplish all He has planned for you and...so do we! There is hope for you and a better future. Believe it!

A ministry friend of mine and one of the endorsers of "Chained No More", Carol Kent, has a son who has been sentenced to life in prison for a murder he committed. Never in a million years did this family think their only child would end up in a prison in Florida, but that is where he will spend the rest of his days. He was a Christian when he committed this crime he thought was justified, but the judge saw it differently. He is now making the most of his circumstances by bringing numerous ministries into his world and has led many to the Lord. His parents travel around the world telling their story and of how the Lord has given them grace and strength through these unthinkable circumstances. Do you see how God can use your pain for good if you will let Him? You have experienced the healing hand of God in "Chained No More" and you may be given the opportunity someday to reach out to someone and give them hope too! How does that sound?

You have the opportunity to begin to restructure your life on many levels: personally, relationally, spiritually, etc. This may be the ending chapter of this book, but it is just the beginning for you and your future today.

Hopefully, through this study, you see how you have let the chains of hurt define you and how the enemy has chained you down with the chains of insecurity and immense damage. The day God brought you to this earth as a little baby, you were not born to have these insecurities. Just to remind you, all the experiences you have had in your life have molded you into who you are today. You may never forget them, but they don't have to have power over you anymore. Remember your "Click Points" from Chapter 10. This is just the beginning of your new perspective on life. One day at a time.

We hope you have experienced strong healing while going through "Chained No More" and that God has revealed many things to you. We pray that you have been honest, open, and vulnerable to His Holy Spirit and have more hope now. Hope for a brighter and healthier future; a future with more joy and strength in God; a future of contentment and peace. A future led by God's perspective and not the perspective you began this journey with.

God's Word is full of statements about who you are and about His plan/purpose for you. Let *Him* be your Guiding Light in this journey now. Look back on the "Identity Theft...Who Am I *Really*?" in Chapter 10 to remember all that God says you are. Yes, those are all about YOU from God's perspective. That is truth and it belongs to YOU.

"Do not conform any longer to the pattern of this world, but be transformed by the renewing of your mind. Then you will be able to test and approve what God's will is – His good, pleasing and perfect will." Romans 12:2

Jackson had been through a lot in his 41 years of life that left him feeling shattered, inferior and hurt. His parents had separated and gone through a very messy divorce, his brother was killed in a car accident, and he had multiple breakups through his teen years and early 20s. He seemed to have trouble keeping good jobs and spent most of his time isolating himself and being afraid to expand his experiences. Oh, he had gone to church sometimes and even tried counseling, but those same feelings of inferiority and sadness kept a cloud over his head. Nothing seemed to help or make a difference for any length of time.

One day, a co-worker began to talk with Jackson about how Jesus healed his own broken and shattered life about two years ago. Stan shared things that Jackson could relate to. It was like he really knew him and could read his mind. Stan knew the pain of divorce, the loss of a loved one and he understood the crushing feeling of depression.

Stan began to share how he gave all his damage, his hurts, his failures and shortcomings to Jesus and how he was changed forever. The power of Stan's past no longer had a hold on him. He shared how he had a new purpose in his life and new self-worth as he finally realized the truth of how God viewed him. He had made changes for a better future and was not going to let the enemy control him anymore. Not only did Stan tell him of his change of heart, but he also shared *how* he made positive changes.

As Stan began to change and live his life in the light of God's Word, His perspective on life changed as well. He was able to set healthier boundaries in his life and those he knew saw these positive changes and all of Stan's relationships improved. He was a happier, more determined man people were now drawn to. What a difference!

"The first step toward change is *awareness*. The second step is *acceptance*. The third step is *action*," Stan said. Oh, Jackson was well aware that his life needed to change and he wanted to accept and experience change. The hard part was stepping out and taking the right actions. He knew what the first step of action needed to be. That evening after work, through buckets of tears, he gave his life to Christ and surrendered all his hurts and failures to God. At that point, Jackson began his journey of change. He would never be the same again.

Rebuilding anything takes a plan, active steps, time and patience. This is your life and rebuilding will take all of these components. After all, it has taken this long to bring you where you are today, and it will take some time to step out of it too. One step at a time. Turn to the Chapter 13 workbook pages. Take some time and ask God to show you the way. He will because He wants you to be whole again and live a life of joy, freedom and strength in Him.

Oh, life will still happen. You will still go through struggles and may slip back occasionally to your old patterns, but now you can go to the Heavenly Father right away. You have the tools to step over the enemy with the strength of God Who truly loves you and He will show you the way out.

Each day is another day of living *"Chained No More"*. May God bless you as you continue your journey. If you find areas that trip you up, please be willing to find a good counselor, pastor, therapist, or chaplain to help you take more steps toward being the best you can be. You can also go back through this book and review to help you get back on track. All of us at Robyn B Ministries wish you a healthy and a successful future, free from the chains of your past. We hope you can enjoy rich, vibrant and healthy relationships and see the positive things in life, no matter where you are at this time in your life.

Here are some excellent resources that can help you continue on your journey to freedom and joy:

- Robyn B Ministries –www.robynbministries.com The author's website includes information on *"Chained No More"*, encouraging blogs, information about Robyn B and how to book her for a concert and/or speaking event.

- "Through the Rain...Crisis to Hope" – www.robynbministries.com/music The accompanying CD to "Chained No More", written and sung by Robyn B, to gently and musically lead you from crisis to hope in Jesus Christ. Sit back and let the songs soothe your soul.
- "A Mind Renewed by God" Email: kimlyndahodge.gmail.com – a powerful book written by Dr. Kimball Hodge that will continue to encourage you and give you tools to move further along on your journey to a healthier life.
- Divorce Care – www.divorcecare.org This ministry has thousands of support groups for those who are or have gone through the devastation of divorce.
- Church Initiative – www.churchinitiative.org. This amazing company has resources for healing from divorce, grief, as well as tools for single parents and their kids.
- AMFM (Association of Marriage and Family Ministries) www.amfmonline.com An extensive network of ministries concerning families
- www.hlp4.com - A website that has many articles concerning various areas of divorce by Linda Jacobs, the developer of Divorce Care For Kids (DC4K)

For other links to encourage you, please go to the link page at www.robynbministries.com

CHAINED
—no
MORE

Workbook Pages

TABLE OF CONTENTS

LINKS IN YOUR CHAIN

(Part One)

IDENTIFYING

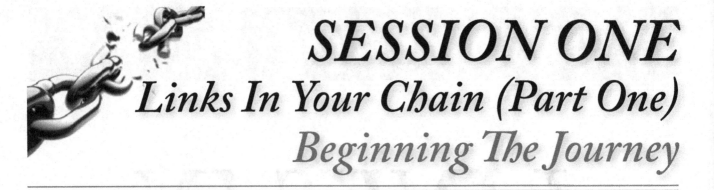

SESSION ONE
Links In Your Chain (Part One)
Beginning The Journey

SESSION GOALS

- See the devastating stats of divorce in the USA
- Learn about the purpose of "Chained No More" and how you can benefit the most from it
- Identify and acknowledge the issues that may have been caused by the divorce of your parents or other childhood brokenness

May the Lord bring you into an ever deeper understanding of the love of God and endurance that comes from Christ. 2 Thess. 3:5

Links of Issues

What are the issues you struggle with at this time in your life? Please fill out this page to help you identify the different issues that have held you back. Mark the issues that you deal with and then put a star by the one or two that you struggle with the most.

_____ **TRUST—**Unable to trust people at their word. Had breakups because of jealousy. Unable to trust men, women, authority figures, and so on.

_____ **FEAR—**Afraid of rejection. Afraid of the dark. Afraid of failure. Afraid of getting hurt. Fear seems to enter into most everything you do.

_____ **ABANDONMENT—**Afraid someone will walk away from you if you don't say or do certain things. Afraid to be alone. Difficult to form long-lasting friendships. Always feel as if you are on the outside looking in.

_____ **BETRAYAL—**Have been let down by others so you don't get involved much. Always waiting to be hurt again. Hatred of gossip. Unable to trust.

_____ **ANGER—**Cannot seem to control your anger. You can verbally or physically attack in an instant. Angry thoughts throughout the day.

_____ **CONFIDENCE—**Don't have a healthy self-image of yourself. See the flaws much more than the positives about yourself. Have difficulty with conversations or speaking in public. Afraid you will be rejected or that you are not good enough.

_____ **FORGIVENESS—**Cannot seem to forgive those who have hurt you and not sure how. Feel that if you forgive, that person is off the hook. The pain is too great to forgive.

_____ **COMMITMENT—**Afraid to make personal commitments to others because you're fearful of being hurt or rejected. Always keep a way out of a commitment possible. Don't want to get too close to others but long for a close relationship.

_____ **DEPRESSION—**Can't seem to get out of the fog. Look at the glass half empty. Nothing ever seems to work out for you. Feel as if you are drowning in a pool of gray. Want to stay in the house and pull the covers up over your head. Loss of interest in things that used to excite you.

_____ **LONELINESS—**Feel isolated and as if no one truly cares about you. Wait for someone to call but can't make the effort to call someone else. Feel as if no one understands you or what you are going through.

_____ **FAITH—**Find it difficult to trust in the Almighty God when you have been through so much. Difficult to have faith and hope that everything will be okay.

Links of Losses

The losses are great for the children of divorce. So much is taken away; some replaced and some taken away forever. Look at the list below and mark the losses that you have experienced as a direct result of the separation/divorce of your parents or other childhood brokenness. Put a star by the losses that have been the most painful for you. Feel free to write notes to explore the reasons for these losses.

_____ A happy, healthy family

_____ Personal identity

_____ Security

_____ Relationships with grandparents

_____ Pets

_____ Friends

_____ School/teachers

_____ Church

_____ A relationship with your dad

_____ A relationship with your mom

_____ A relationship with your brothers/sisters

_____ A healthy childhood

_____ Financial stability

_____ Trust in people

_____ Holiday/birthday traditions

_____ House and significant items from the loss of it

Hopefully, by filling these pages out, you will be able to see the "before picture" of yourself (before completing "Chained No More"). All of us have "stuff", so please be patient with yourself and be open to God's healing. You are on your way!

LINKS IN YOUR CHAIN
(Part Two)

IDENTIFYING

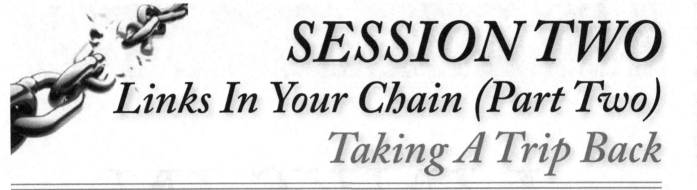

SESSION TWO
Links In Your Chain (Part Two)
Taking A Trip Back

SESSION GOALS

* Look back to the crisis and trauma of your parents' separation/divorce
* Explore your experience, how it affected those involved, and the emotions involved
* Look at the possible family patterns of marriage and divorce in your immediate and extended family and how they may affect you

Remember, O Lord, Your great mercy and love, for they are from of old. Remember not the sins of my youth and my rebellious ways; according to Your love, remember me, for You are good. O Lord. Psalm 25:6,7

The Chains of Your Parents' Divorce

The divorce of parents can often begin bringing devastation and damage to children, following them all their lives. Going back and recognizing the effect your parents' divorce may have had on you can be a beginning step to a brighter future, allowing you to be free of the heavy chains from it. If your parents were not divorced, you can answer the questions about your own divorce or the death of a parent, if you would like to.

Year of your parents' divorce _____ How old were you then? _____

Did you see it coming? _____
_____

How did you learn that they were separating? _____
_____

What do you remember about that conversation/revelation? _____
_____
_____
_____

How did you feel? _____

What was your reaction? _____
_____

Did someone comfort you? _____ Who? _____

How? _____

How long after that did the one parent move out? _____

Were you there when your parent moved out? _____

Was it a one-time event or was there a lot of going back and forth/moving in and out? _____
_____

With whom did you live? _____

How was that decided? _____

Were you able to see both parents? _____

Why or why not? _____

_____

If so, how often?_____

Were you able to live with your siblings? _____

_____

How long was it before your parents went to court? _____

_____

During the process, how would you describe your parents' relationship or communication? _____

_____

_____

Were you kept informed about what was going on in court? _____

_____

By who? _____

What emotions began to surface? _____

_____

Did your behavior begin to change? _____

If so, how? (For example, fighting, isolation, lower school grades, depression, and so forth) _____

_____

_____

_____

The Chains of Childhood Brokenness

For those of you who are not from a divorced family or have experienced your own divorce, this alternate page is for you. Trauma and crisis in childhood can be the beginning of issues that will last a lifetime. Think as far back as you can about traumatic experiences that happened and fill out the page below.

What was the trauma/crisis? _____

_____

How old were you? _____

Did you see it coming? _____

How did it make you feel? _____

How did you react? _____

Did you tell anyone? _____ Why or why not? _____

_____

What was their response?_____

Did anyone comfort you? _____ Who? _____

How did they comfort you? _____

Was this a one-time event or not? _____

If not, how often did it occur? _____

What emotions do you feel now in remembering it?_____

_____

How do you think it has affected you? _____

_____

Family Footprints

If your parent(s) remarried, do you remember the day your parent told you that he or she was going to get married to someone else? Do you remember the feelings you had? Were you happy, scared, angry, or did you just dismiss it? Most parents will date and marry again—some successfully and some unsuccessfully.

Please fill out the page below to explore only that which applies to your story. To remind you, you may transfer these questions to your own marriages, if you wish.

MOTHER
How many times has your mother been married? _____

First remarriage—year your mother married again: _____ until _____
Write your thoughts on that marriage:

Second remarriage—year your mother married again: _____ until _____
Write your thoughts on that marriage:

Third remarriage—Year your mother married again: _____ until _____
Write your thoughts on that marriage:

FATHER
How many times has your father been married? _____

First remarriage—year your father married again: _____ until _____
Write your thoughts on that marriage:

Second remarriage—year your father married again: _____ until _____
Write your thoughts on that marriage:

Third remarriage—year your father married again: _____ until _____
Write your thoughts on that marriage:

UNDERSTANDING THE LINKS

CONNECTIONS

SESSION THREE
Understanding The Links
The Chain Of Grief

SESSION GOALS

- Begin to look at the "Chain of Grief"
- Recognize where you think you are at this point on that chain
- Explore the denial and bargaining portion of the "Chain of Grief" and see how you may have used these in the past and may still be using them today
- Look at the subjects of betrayal and trust and how they may still be playing out in your life today

Teach me Your way, O Lord; and I will walk in Your truth;
give me an undivided heart, that I may fear You. Psalm 86:11

Chain of Grief

The breakup of a family is reason for grief and all the emotions that are part of that. At the beginning of your parents' separation, you might have lived in denial and believed that everything would be okay. Maybe you began to bargain with your parents, yourself, or God. (For instance, *"If I get better grades, maybe my parents will be happier and won't divorce."*) Maybe you were buried by anger when you realized that there was nothing you could do about your family crisis. Depression is a large part of the grief cycle, and you may have lived with depression for quite some time; you may even still be struggling with it at times.

You may have processed many emotions already, and some you may have not faced yet. Processing through the chain of grief can take a long time, and you may slip back and forth between links. Everyone deals with grief differently, so there is no "normal" way. Take your time. Study the chain below and feel free to add your own emotions on it. Please put an X beside where you are today on the grief cycle concerning the divorce of your parents, or if your parent (s) remarried and divorced again. You may also choose to address other chains from other crisis in your life, such as the death of a loved one, your own divorce, loss of a relationship, etc. You may also put an X by where you are concerning those and then label each one.

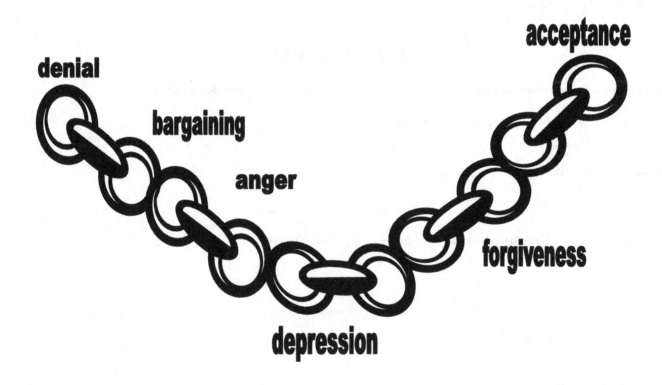

REMINDER: Although the above emotions are general ones, you may write additional ones such as guilt, shame, embarrassment surrender, etc.

Chain of Grief:
Denial and Bargaining

When your parents first said they were getting a separation/divorce, did you deny that it was happening because you hoped it wouldn't? Did you think you could bargain it away? Remember that you can adapt this to other chains you wrote about on the previous page.

DENIAL: *"There is no way this is going to happen. They will work it out."*

BARGAINING: *"Maybe if I get better grades and clean my room, they won't fight so much and won't divorce." "Maybe I could invite both of my parents out to dinner and it could rekindle their love for each other."*

Getting stuck in denial can keep you from facing the reality of a situation. It can stop you from processing through healing from the start.

Getting stuck in bargaining can keep you unsuccessfully trying to prevent what is going to happen anyway and keep you from accepting a situation.

WHAT ABOUT YOU?

How much of the pain from your parents' separation/divorce have you handled with denial? (0-100%) _____

In what other areas of your life have you used denial? _____
_____

How did it change the reality of the situation? _____
_____
_____

In what ways did you try to bargain/manipulate during your parents' divorce? _____
_____
_____

How did it change the situation? _____
_____
_____

Have you ever tried to bargain with God about something? _____

How did it work? _____
_____
_____
_____

Betrayal / Trust

What does trust mean to you? _____

_____

How easy is it for you to trust people? _____

_____

How does this play out in your life? _____

_____

How does a person build trust? _____

_____

How does a person lose trust? _____

_____

Who do you feel has betrayed you in your life? List any names here, putting an X by those you believe you have truly forgiven:

_____ _____ _____

_____ _____ _____

In what relationship(s) would you like to rebuild trust? How can you begin to rebuild your trust with those people?

_____

_____

God's Idea of Trust

Trust means believing in someone or depending on them. Sometimes it means trusting them to help us out in life, especially in a time of crisis or need. *Only* the Lord is worthy of absolute trust. Because God can be trusted, His Word is also trustworthy, and we can depend on it.

All too often, however, we put our trust in other people to help us out in times of trouble, but the Bible warns us that other people can and often will disappoint and fail us. Security is never to be found ultimately in other people or in things; it can only be found in a relationship with the Lord, Who brings freedom and fullness as we trust in Him.

If our trust in others is broken by their own brokenness, we can still have a solid foundation of God's love and faithfulness.

 # FROM GOD'S WORD

The Lord is good, a refuge in times of trouble. He cares for those who trust in Him. (Nah. 1:7)

Trust in the Lord with all your heart and lean not on your own understanding; in all your ways acknowledge Him and He will make your paths straight. (Prov. 3:5)

Many are the woes of the wicked, but the Lord's unfailing love surrounds the man who trusts in Him. (Ps. 32:10)

We wait in hope for the Lord; He is our help and our shield. In Him our hearts rejoice, for we trust in His holy name. May Your unfailing love rest upon us, O Lord, even as we put our hope in You. (Ps. 33:20-22)

POWER OF THE CHAIN

"His divine power has given us everything we need for life and godliness through our knowledge of Him who called us by His own glory and goodness, through these He has given us His very great and precious promises, so that through them, you may participate in the divine nature and escape the corruption in the world caused by evil desires" (2 Peter 1:3–4).

SESSION FOUR
Power Of The Chain
Family Patterns And Their Effects

 **SESSION GOALS**

- Explore your family's patterns of divorce or other childhood trauma
- Look at the issues in your family, how they dealt or deal with them, and then see how you have continued or broken those patterns in your personal life
- Look at the positive/negative effects your parents have had on you
- Explore the issue of keeping secrets and lies concerning your parents' divorce and the effect it has on you today
- Look at what was/is your fault and what was/is not, as well as what is in your control and out of your control

Turn my eyes away from worthless things; preserve
my life according to Your Word. —Ps. 119:37

Family

The rate of divorce has increased over the years and many times goes from generation to generation in a family. How about yours? Who in your family tree has been divorced?

_____ PARENTS   Approx. years married _____

_____ GRANDPARENTS   Approx. years married _____

_____ GRANDPARENTS   Approx. years married _____

_____ AUNT/UNCLE   Approx. years married _____

_____ AUNT/UNCLE   Approx. years married _____

_____ SIBLING   Approx. years married _____

_____ SIBLING   Approx. years married _____

_____ CHILD   Approx. years married _____

_____ CHILD   Approx. years married _____

_____ OTHER   Approx. years married _____

_____ OTHER   Approx. years married _____

How many times has your mom been divorced? _____

How many times has your dad been divorced? _____

Name people in your life who have been married for over twenty years and never been divorced: _____

_____

_____

Why do you think it works for them? _____

_____

_____

Living in the House: Family Patterns

To understand the links in your family chains, you must recognize the behavior patterns, acknowledge them, see the influence they had over you, and understand how they have affected your life. Once you understand the links, you can then decide what changes you want to make.

Some patterns are positive, such as encouragement, laughter, taking personal responsibility, and handling frustration in a healthy way. Some patterns are negative, such as yelling, stomping out of the room, ignoring the situation, belittling others, physical abuse, and so forth.

Please fill out the page below as you recognize some of the patterns you had in your house, including which person you had the issue with, how the family dealt with that person/issue and how it has influenced your life as an adult.

EXAMPLE:

MAKING PROMISES—Person involved: Dad
Family pattern: Never trusted his word; just "wait and see"
Personal pattern: Conscientious about keeping my word and always being on time

CONFLICT/CONFRONTATION—Person involved: _____

Family pattern: _____

Personal pattern: _____

INTEGRITY/HONESTY—Person involved: _____

Family pattern: _____

Personal pattern: _____

KEEPING HOME CLEAN—Person involved: _____

Family pattern: _____

Personal pattern: _____

DISCIPLINE—Person involved: _____

Family pattern: _____

Personal pattern: _____

HEALTHY LIFESTYLE—Person involved: _____

Family pattern: _____

Personal pattern: _____

What About Parenting?

We are all a product of our parenting, good or bad. Some of us had a healthy upbringing, while many of us lived in dysfunctional homes where stress and conflict were a normal way of life.

What are some of the ways your upbringing has affected your life so far? Please fill out the section below and identify which of the parenting behaviors apply to you. Dig deep so you can get the most out of it. Upon completing this page, put a star by the patterns you have broken or want to break in your own life.

NOTE: This is *not* meant to be about blaming your parents for their behaviors or their decisions in life. This is just to identify how your childhood may have affected you.

PARENTING	EFFECT ON YOU
Parents yelling at each other	
Parent leaving the family	
Giving you all you wanted	
Your sibling being "the favorite"	
Verbal abuse	
Strict religiously	
No religion/faith	
Discouraging/encouraging words	
Not being involved in your activities/sports	
Physical violence in the home	
Drug/alcohol abuse	
Being lied to	
Broken promises	
Caring grandparents	
Never good enough	

Secrets and Lies

Many kids who live through the divorce of their parents are expected to keep secrets, be message carriers, act as spies, and lie for their parents through the battle of divorce. Please fill out the page below as you explore these issues.

If you went to visit a parent, were you "interrogated" after the visit by your other parent? _____

If so, how did it make you feel? _____

_____

How did you deal with it? _____

_____

Did your parent(s) ask you to lie to your other parent? _____

What were some of the things you were told to lie about? _____

_____

Did you feel you had a choice? _____ How did you deal with this issue? _____

_____

Were you expected to keep secrets between your parents? _____ What kinds of secrets? _____

_____

Was it difficult for you to keep the lies and secrets straight between your parents?

_____

_____

Explain:

Do you think keeping secrets and lying for your parents has affected your life as you have grown? _____

How? _____

_____

_____

Mark the challenges you have with these issues as you have become an adult:

_____ Tend to be able to tell believable lies

_____ Difficulty keeping things confidential

_____ Difficulty trusting the word of other people

_____ Cynical a lot of the time

_____ Confident that people are all liars

_____ Find it easy to blame others

_____ Tend to choose friends who are straight up

_____ Find yourself being very blunt sometimes

_____ Find that you almost interrogate people about things

_____ Afraid to make a commitment because you might be lied to

_____ Don't believe anything people tell you

_____ Don't feel safe enough in relationships to be honest and open

_____ Keep people at arm's length emotionally and physically

_____ Constantly searching for anyone to fill the void

_____ Find yourself prone to gossiping because of anger inside or feeling as if you have to be the "secret holder"

_____ Get defensive whenever anyone asks you too many questions

Do you see how these issues have followed you throughout your life? How can you make some positive steps to break these patterns and be free of them? Look at each issue and beside each one, write the steps you may be able to take.

SESSION FIVE
Grip Of The Chain
Recognizing Anger

SESSION GOALS

- Focus on getting a grip on your anger before it grips *you*
- Identify your reactions of anger as well as what sets you off
- Discuss your anger at God and how you can deal with that
- Find healthy ways to diffuse your anger

My dear brother, take note of this; everyone should be quick to listen, slow to speak, and slow to become angry, for man's anger does NOT bring about the righteous life that God desires. —James 1:19-20

Write down some words that describe the different levels of anger.

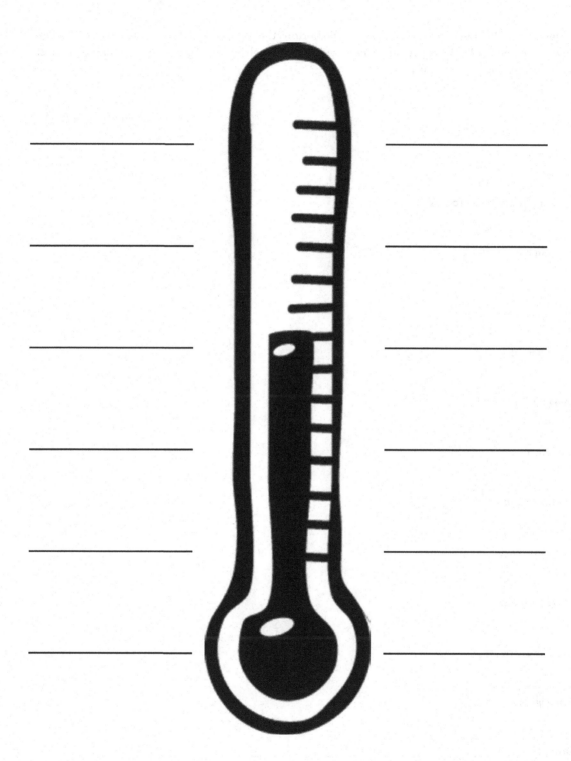

_____

_____

_____

_____

_____

_____

Now circle the level of anger that you may be experiencing in your life today.

What Ticks You Off?

Everyone gets angry at times, and everyone has certain buttons that people push that can make us angry. Please fill out the page below and explore what ticks you off. Think about why the highest scoring ones make you the angriest because you may find some more links to your chain.

Level of Anger (1-5)

_____ Being lied to   _____

_____ Someone breaking a promise   _____

_____ Issues in our country   _____

_____ Injustice   _____

_____ A bad hair day   _____

_____ Being misunderstood   _____

_____ Favoritism   _____

_____ Wrongly accused   _____

_____ Someone leaving you   _____

_____ Being yelled at   _____

_____ Being disrespected   _____

_____ Being ignored   _____

_____ Other _____   _____

Link of Truth

Anger can be a tricky emotion because it can sneak up on you or sit and smolder for a long time before you feel it strongly.

One day you think you are over an offense and have forgiven the person, and all of a sudden, something triggers your anger. Maybe it is a smell or the taste of something. Maybe you see that person again and all the memories come flooding back—and you find that it still has a strong power over you.

There will always be conflict and differences of opinions. There will always be two sides to a story, and there will always be people who feel they need to win an argument. We usually vent our anger to the person we trust the most. Unfortunately, it is most likely a family member; something to contemplate and change.

As far as adult children of divorce are concerned, there may have been many years of built-up anger because of the breakup of the family. Pushing it aside is not the answer; making everyone else pay for it is not the answer either.

The answer is to face it head-on and look at the issues, see the painful power it has over you, seek healing, learn to forgive (chapter 9), and become free from the anger that has gripped you.

We can't help the first thought we have, but we sure can help the second and third and whether we dwell on them. At the first sign of anger, we have a decision as to how we are going to respond. We have the choice of whether or not to be in control.

Let's get started!

Signs of Anger

It is important to know what pushes your buttons, but it also helps to know what your first signs of anger are so you can identify them and control your anger sooner rather than later. Which of these do you experience?

_____ Gritting teeth

_____ Tightening shoulders

_____ Making fists

_____ Yelling

_____ Hitting

_____ Falling silent

_____ Turning and walking away

_____ Isolating yourself

_____ Raising your eyebrows

_____ Breathing deeper

_____ Tighten lips

_____ Blaming self

_____ Grunting or making other noises

_____ Folding arms

_____ Self-medicating (e.g., using TV, drugs, alcohol, books, food, sex)

_____ Slamming doors

_____ Throwing things

Now, consider why you have these reactions. Were they family patterns while you were growing up? More chains.

Are some of them acceptable to you? Are there some you desire to change? Are some harmful to you or others?

Managing Your Anger

Here are some ways to release angry feelings in a healthy and safe way. Look at the list below and check the ones you have used in the past. Now look at the list again and circle the ones you would be willing to try:

- Exercise.

- Take a long, slow walk.

- Cry.

- Determine if this is something within your control or not.

- Talk about it with a person you can trust (a friend, teacher, pastor, counselor, family member), someone who is a good listener.

- Close your eyes, breathe deeply, and let yourself feel angry until it slowly begins to fade away.

- If you are angry, don't watch violent movies, play violent computer/video games, or listen to loud music. They may influence you, increasing the anger or causing you to act out in destructive ways.

- Take a hot bath or a cold shower, whatever "cools" you down.

- Work on any kind of puzzle or problem that needs solving. This can serve as a great distraction and keep your mind busy.

- Listen to some relaxing music.

- Sing uplifting and positive songs.

- Write a letter or write in your journal.

- Do anything that calms you down. Go to the park. Watch the sun set, gaze at the moon, sit by a lake or the ocean.

- Talk to God aloud about the issues you are angry about. Lay it all out to Him (He knows it anyway!). In doing this, you will not only be communicating with Him, but you will also be able to hear yourself and the anger you carry rather than denying it.

- Learn to hold your tongue and think before you speak. Staying in control of yourself is important.

- Read the scriptures concerning anger and keeping peace in obedience to His Word.

ANGER: Three Ways to Deal with It

(Adapted from *The Big D... Divorce Thru the Eyes of a Teen - by Krista Smith*)

1. **TAKING IT OUT ON OTHERS—**This aggressive way of dealing with anger includes hitting, screaming, cussing, accusing others, putting others down, damaging property, and so on. It is destructive, tends to hurt others, and resolves little. Aggressive anger is often directed toward "safe" people, such as family members or friends.

2. **HOLDING IT IN—**You can passively bottle your feelings by not talking about them. Anger still comes out in pouting and withdrawing as the person tries to punish others, but it usually hurts the angry person the most.

3. **TALKING IT OUT—**This is the assertive way: honestly and openly telling others that you feel mad—and why. You can be animated and loud or soft and reasonable. When we talk out our anger, we move through it and don't have to stay angry too long.

Be ... quick to listen, slow to speak and slow to become angry ...
—James 1:19-20

God's Word on Anger

Is anger wrong? If it is wrong, why did God create this emotion? How can we use this emotion effectively without offending others?

God has a lot to say about the emotion of anger and is clear in His Word about the boundaries we should use, whether we are just a little "ticked off" or feeling rage. He wants us to control our anger, leaving revenge and justice to Him.

Dr. Kimball Hodge says, "Ephesians 4:26–27 is a fantastic verse on anger. The Greek language says 'Be angry,,,.' In the NIV, it says, 'In your anger do not sin.' The 'be angry' can be productive (anger can resolve situations, producing determination or motivation). It can also become destructive when it is misdirected (for instance, bitterness turning into resentment, wrath, and rage)."

Verse 27 says, "Don't let the sun go down while you are still angry," which means deal with it and resolve it. This may mean settling things with God first before you go to bed at night, even if you have not resolved the situation with someone else at that point.

 ## FROM GOD'S WORD

A gentle answer turns away wrath, but a harsh word stirs up anger. (Prov. 15:1)

A fool gives full vent to his anger, but a wise man keeps himself under control. (Ps. 29:11)

In your anger do not sin. Do not let the sun go down while you are still angry and do not give the devil a foothold. (Eph. 4:26–27)

An angry man stirs up dissension and a hot-tempered one commits many sins. A man's pride brings him low, but a man of lowly spirit gains honor. (Prov. 29:22–23)

UNDER THE GRIP OF THE CHAIN

WHAT'S REALLY GOING ON?

SESSION SIX
Under The Grip Of The Chain
Exploring What Is Behind Anger

 **SESSION GOALS**

- Learn what is *really* under all that anger
- Become familiar with the names of many emotions
- Identify the worries you felt because of your parents' divorce and other trauma
- Identify the emotions you are feeling and release your pain

The Lord is a shelter for the oppressed, a refuge in time of trouble.
Those who know Your name trust in You, for You, O Lord, have
never abandoned anyone who searches for You. —Ps. 9:9-10

Anger Umbrella

Anger is an emotion that covers up other feelings you are also experiencing. Everyone gets angry, but with a closer look, you might find the emotions of frustration, sadness, betrayal, fear, abandonment, hurt, and so forth. It is important to recognize these feelings so you can deal with them in a healthy way. Let's try it ...

LAST TIME YOU WERE ANGRY:

Who or what: _____

Reason: _____

_____

_____

DIG DEEP

What were some other emotions you were feeling? _____

_____

_____

SITUATION #2

Who or what: _____

Reason: _____

_____

_____

Other emotions: _____

_____

_____

SITUATON #3

Who or what: _____

Reason: _____

_____

_____

Other emotions: _____

_____

_____

SITUATON #4

Who or what: _____

Reason: _____

_____

_____

Other emotions: _____

_____

_____

Doing this activity will hopefully help you identify emotions sooner and help you resolve them more effectively now and in the future.

Worry, Worry, Worry

Stress and worry are parts of our everyday lives and can cause health problems, lack of concentration, loss of relationships and jobs, and so on. Many times, stress and worry are behind the anger that we feel.

Can you remember when you were a little kid, before your parents' separation/divorce or other painful experiences, how carefree you may have been?

Now can you remember how worried and confused you were when your family split apart? Identify some of the things you worried about during that time in your life. You may also add additional things you worried about as a child. It will show you the weight that worry had on you as a kid. You may also consider the same hurts your own kids felt when you divorced.

Where would I live?

Would I see both of my parents?

Would I have to change schools?

Would we be poor?

Would my parents stop loving *me* too?

Was the divorce my fault?

Would I get divorced in my life?

What would the judge say about our family?

Would other kids make fun of me or ignore me?

Would I still get to see my grandparents?

What would happen during holidays/celebrations?

Who would decide where I lived?

What if my mom or dad remarried?

What would I tell my friends?

What effects has worry had on you?

_____

_____

What do you worry about today?

_____

_____

"Cast all your anxiety on Him because He cares for you." I Peter 5:7

WEIGHT OF THE CHAIN

DEPRESSION

SESSION SEVEN
Weight Of The Chain
Facing Depression

SESSION GOALS

- Explore depression—what it is and what it looks like
- Look at the different levels of depression and recognize where you are
- Consider healthy and unhealthy ways to cope with depression

"May our Lord Jesus Christ Himself and God our Father, who loved us and by His grace gave us eternal encouragement and good hope, encourage your hearts and strengthen you in every good deed and word." —2 Thess. 2:16-17

Weight of the Chain: Depression

Depression comes in many forms and behaviors. Look at the depression chain below and rate yourself where you are today. Check as many as apply. Add more if you wish. Note: If you are not experiencing depression presently, go back and think of a time when you were.

CRYING _____

LACKING MOTIVATION _____

LACKING ENERGY _____

OVER/UNDEREATING _____

SLEEPING TOO MUCH/TOO LITTLE _____

ONLY SEEING THE NEGATIVE _____

GIVING UP _____

ISOLATING _____

BEING SUICIDAL _____

Reasons for Your Depression

Please make a list of why you may be feeling any level of depression you checked on the previous page.

_____

_____

_____

_____

_____

_____

_____

_____

_____

_____

_____

_____

_____

_____

Depression and You

You may wake up one day and feel a little sad and down, and sometimes depression can sneak up on you and make you realize that it is affecting several areas of your life. Depression can sometimes make you feel as if you are drowning and can't see a way out, or it can sometimes manifest as anger. Sound familiar?

1. How depressed are you feeling today? _____

2. On page 45, where are you on the depression chain? _____

3. How long have you been at that level? _____

4. Do you take medication for depression? _____

5. Do you feel it is working? _____

6. Do you see a professional about this? _____ If so, how is it helpful to you? _____

_____

7. How is depression affecting your life? (Check all that you are experiencing)

_____ general feeling of sadness
_____ nothing seems fun anymore
_____ lack of concentration
_____ withdrawing/isolating from my friends
_____ want to stay in bed with the covers pulled up
_____ not sleeping well
_____ not eating well
_____ difficulty with concentration/memory
_____ difficulty making everyday decisions
_____ affecting my relationships
_____ affecting my walk with God
_____ angry feelings

"As the deer pants for streams of water, so my soul pants for You, O God, for the living God. When can I go and meet with God? My tears have been my food day and night, while men say to me all day long, 'Where is your God?' These things I remember as I pour out my soul; how I used to go with the multitude leading the procession to the house of God, with shouts of joy and thanksgiving among the festive throng. Why are you downcast, O my soul? Why so disturbed within me? Put your hope in God, for I will yet praise Him, my Savior and my God." —Ps. 42:1-5a

Depression: What Do You Do?

We all get depressed at some point in our lives—from feeling slightly depressed to experiencing debilitating depression. To help you see a brighter day, what do you do when you begin to get depressed? Which ones are effective? Which are not? Which ones may be actually "feeding" your depression?

WHEN I FEEL BLUE:

People I talk to: _____

_____

Places I go: _____

_____

Music I listen to: _____

_____

Books I read: _____

_____

Projects I do: _____

_____

Physical activities I do: _____

_____

Movies/TV shows I watch: _____

_____

Scriptures I read: _____

_____

These are ways you can "nurture yourself" when headed into depression. At the first sign of feeling down, implement one or more. Looking at the list above. What do you need to adjust, eliminate, or add?

_____

_____

God Understands Depression

Do God's people suffer discouragement, depression, and even despair? Yes, as various examples in the Bible indicate, some of the greatest characters in the Bible experienced depression, and on some occasions, they were so depressed that they expressed the desire to die. Many of the Psalms, including Psalm 13:1-2, 31:9-11, and 42:9-10, honestly unveil human anguish and hurt. These intense emotions, often accompanied by a sense of sadness and hopelessness, are a natural human reaction to the stresses and losses that are common to life.

God's foremost answer when we experience these emotions is to remind us that He is with us through the Holy Spirit, and that we can restore our confidence and hope through Him and in Him. At the same time, we can often receive strength and encouragement from the support, love, and concern of other believers.

 ## FROM GOD'S WORD

Be strong and take heart, all you who hope in the Lord. (Ps. 31:24)

Why are you downcast, O my soul? Why so disturbed within me? Put your hope in God, for I will yet praise Him, my Savior and my God. (Ps. 42:11)

Humble yourselves, therefore, under God's mighty hand, that He may lift you up in due time. Cast all your anxiety on Him because He cares for you." (I Pet. 5:6-7)

GOD'S LINK TO YOU

"The Lord is the shelter for the oppressed, a refuge in time of trouble. Those who know Your name trust in You, for You, O Lord, have never abandoned anyone who searches for You."
(Psalm 9:9–10)

SESSION EIGHT
God's Link To You
Who God Is To You

 **SESSION GOALS**

- Define who you are aside from the past
- Explore who God is to you and where you learned it
- Compare your earthly parents to God, the Heavenly Father, through the truth of His Word
- Write a letter to God

I will praise You because I am fearfully and wonderfully made;
Your works are wonderful, I know that full well. —Ps. 139:14

Chained No More

God and You

Who is God to you? Do you even believe that there *is* a God? Do you pray to Him? Do you seek His Word for wisdom and clarity in your life? Have you accepted His Son, Jesus, to be your Savior? Do you know what that means?

Take a few minutes to explore where you are with Him today and what He means to you.

How would you describe God? _____

_____

_____

What was the religious or spiritual life like in your family when you were a child? _____

_____

_____

How is your religious/spiritual life the same as it was in your original family? _____

_____

_____

How is it different? _____

_____

_____

Do you believe in Jesus Christ? Why or why not? _____

_____

_____

If you have accepted Christ, how old were you when you did? _____

Do you believe that God loves you? Do you *feel* His love for you or just *know* about it?

_____

_____

??WHO'S YOUR DADDY??

It can be difficult for people whose parents have hurt them time and time again to be able to trust them again, although many times they wish they could. Now transfer that mistrust to trying to trust our Heavenly Father. "Why should I trust a Heavenly Father I can't see when I can't trust one I can?" Sound familiar? Look at the comparisons between a human parent and the **truth** of our "Heavenly Parent":

Human parent	Heavenly Father
Broken promises	Let us hold unswervingly to the hope we profess, for He who promised is faithful. (Heb. 10:23)
Walked away	I will NEVER leave you nor forsake you. (Heb. 13:5b)
Put me down	But You, O Lord, are a compassionate and gracious God, slow to anger, abounding in love and faithfulness. (Exod. 34:6)
Favored my sibling(s) over me	Here I am! I stand at the door and knock. If ANYONE hears my voice and opens the door, I will come in and eat with him and he with Me. (Rev. 3:20)
Betrayed my other parent	For great is His love toward us, and the FAITHFULNESS of the Lord endures forever. (Ps. 17:2)
Was an addict of some kind	He is the Rock, His works are perfect, and all His ways are just. A faithful God who does no wrong; upright and just is He. (Deut. 32:4)
Punished me physically	God disciplines us for our good, that we may share in His holiness. (Heb. 12:10)
Did not protect me	He is a shield for all who take refuge in Him. For who is God besides the Lord? And who is the Rock except our God? (Ps. 18:30b–31)
Abused me in any way	Peace I leave with you; My peace I give you. I do not give to you as the world gives. Do not let your hearts be troubled and do not be afraid." (John 14:27)
Did not value me	For God so loved the world that He gave His only begotten Son, that whosoever believes in Him should not perish but have eternal life." John 3:16
Lied to me	As for God, His way is perfect; the Word of the Lord is flawless. Ps. 18:30a
Treated me like a slave	It is for freedom that Christ has set us free. Stand firm, then and do not let yourselves be burdened again by a yoke of slavery. (Gal. 5:1)
Was never there for me	"For I know the plans I have for you," declares the Lord, "plans to prosper you and not to harm you, plans to give you hope and a future. (Jer. 29:11)
Spent little time with me	Though my father and my mother forsake me, the Lord will receive me. (Ps. 27:10)
Didn't really listen to me	You will call upon Me and come and pray to Me and I will listen to You. You will seek Me and find Me when you seek Me with all your heart. (Jer. 29:12-13)

Remember: Your parents have/had their own issues in life and are/were as flawed as you are. They have past hurts that they may have passed onto you and never healed from. Their hurts were not about you, but certainly affected you. Take some time to absorb this realization. Our Heavenly Father is the only Perfect One.

God's Care for You

Many of us have grown up not feeling valued. We didn't have that encouragement and support that we longed for so much. You may have felt neglected and as if nobody cared whether you lived or died.

Well, friend, God cares. He created you with gifts and talents, and He has a perfect plan for you. He values you and loves you more than you can ever imagine. Look at what His Word says about you.

 FROM GOD'S WORD
Please read this slowly and out loud. Emphasize the bolded words. This is the truth about you!

*O Lord, You have searched me and **You know me**. You know when I sit
and when I rise; You perceive my thoughts from afar. You discern my going
out and my lying down; You are familiar with **all** my ways.*

*Before a word is on my tongue, **You know it completely**, O Lord.*

*You hem me in—behind and before; **You have laid Your hand upon me**.
Such knowledge is too wonderful for me; too lofty for me to attain.*

*Where can I go from Your Spirit? Where can I flee from Your presence? If I go up to the
heavens, **You are there**; if I make my bed in the depths, **You are there**. If I rise on the wings
of the dawn; if I settle on the far side of the sea, even there **Your Hand will hold me fast**.*

*You created my inmost being; You knitted me together in my mother's womb. I praise You
because I am fearfully and wonderfully made; **Your works are wonderful**; I know that
full well. My frame was not hidden from You when I was made in the secret place. When
I was woven together in the depths of the earth, Your eyes saw my unformed body.*

All the days ordained for me were written in Your book before one of them came to be.

*Search me, O God, and know my heart; test me and know my anxious thoughts.
See if there is any offensive way in me and lead me in the way everlasting.*

(Portions of Psalm 139)

LETTING GO OF THE CHAIN

FORGIVENESS

SESSION NINE
Letting Go Of The Chain
Receiving And Giving Forgiveness

SESSION GOALS

- Explore and define what forgiveness is and what it isn't
- Discover the depth of God's forgiveness for you
- Look at areas of your life where unforgiveness has chained you down
- Break the chain of unforgiveness in your life
- Experience God's grace and be able to give grace to others

Bear with each other and forgive whatever grievances you may have against one another. Forgive as the Lord forgave you. —Colossians 3:13

How do You Spell
F-O-R-G-I-V-E-N-E-S-S?

Please write a word or phrase that reflects your thoughts/beliefs, beginning with each letter of the word "forgiveness."

F

O

R

G

I

V

E

N

E

S

S

Forgiveness: Right or Wrong?

Please look at the following quotes and indicate whether you agree or disagree. Please take time to contemplate each quote.

AGREE	DISAGREE	QUOTE
		"Strength of character means the ability to overcome resentment against others, to hide hurt feelings and to forgive quickly."
		"One of the secrets to a long and fruitful life is to forgive everybody everything before you go to bed."
		"To forgive is to set a prisoner free and discover that the prisoner was *you!*"
		"Two persons cannot be friends for long if they cannot forgive each other's little failings."
		"When a deep injury is done to us, we never recover until we forgive."
		"You must have been given forgiveness to give forgiveness to someone else."
		"He who is devoid of the power to forgive is devoid of the power to fully love."

Is it easy for you to forgive? Why or why not? _____

_____

What has been the most challenging thing you've had to forgive someone for? _____

_____

_____

Forgiveness: Fact or Fiction?

Put a "T" or "F" for each statment:

_____ Forgiving someone means that you will no longer get angry or have any more negative feelings.

_____ If you forgive, you have to put it all behind you and leave it in the past, becoming friends with the person who hurt you.

_____ You do not have to forgive an immoral person.

_____ You may want to forgive someone, but you may not be ready on the inside.

_____ Forgiving is necessary in the healing process, and you will not be able to completely heal until you do so.

_____ You cannot forgive until the offender asks for forgiveness or shows that he or she is sorry.

_____ When you forgive others, you believe and accept that God has forgiven you.

_____ If you forgive someone, you have to forget what that person has done.

_____ Forgiveness depends on getting a guarantee that someone won't do the same wrong thing again.

_____ Forgiveness is unconditional.

_____ Forgiveness excuses the other person's sin or wrongdoing.

(Adapted from *The Big D...Divorce Thru the Eyes of a Teen*, by Krista Smith)

God's Forgiveness To You

If we confess our sins, He is faithful and just and will forgive us
our sins and purify us from all unrighteousness.
(I John 1:9)

Working through forgiveness is one of the most difficult things you may have to do in your journey of healing. In order for us to truly forgive someone, we need to understand and experience God's forgiveness for us. Do you believe that God's Word is Truth? _____ All of it? _____

The Bible says that God sent His only Son, Jesus, to be cruelly beaten and nailed to a cross long ago so that you would not have to pay the penalty of death for the sins you commit. What is your response to this?

_____

_____

Have you accepted God's forgiveness for you from *all* your sins—past, present, and future? _____

_____

Do you believe He won't forgive these sins? _____ If so, why? _____

_____

Looking back on your life so far, looking at all the sins you have committed and the people you have hurt, do you believe that God has forgiven you and keeps no record of wrong?

_____

_____

What sins do you believe you have done that you fear God cannot or will not forgive? _____

_____

_____

For all have sinned and fall short of the glory of God and are justified freely
by His grace through the redemption that came by Christ Jesus.
(Romans 3:23-23)

God's Truths on Forgiveness

It is difficult for humans to truly understand God's idea of forgiveness. We would rather write somebody off if that person has severely hurt us, right? After all, why set ourselves up for more hurt? That person doesn't deserve to be forgiven. Wait a minute! That is not God's idea of forgiveness. He is extremely specific as to how He would have us deal with the issue of forgiveness.

Because of God's compassion, love, grace, and mercy, He offers pardon for our sins by putting them out of sight, out of reach, out of mind, and out of existence. Christ's shedding of His blood on the cross is the ultimate sacrifice, and that loving act took all our sins, all the selfishness, the hatred, the deceit, and the pride and nailed them to the cross so that those who believe might be declared innocent and free from sin's controlling power. He asks us to forgive others as well, although it doesn't mean we need to make the ultimate sacrifice as He did. How can we refuse?

Hopefully, you have learned what forgiveness is and is not through this session. Now let's look a little deeper.

 ## FROM GOD'S WORD

If You, O Lord, kept a record of sins, O Lord, who could stand? But with You, there is forgiveness; therefore You are feared. (Ps. 130:3-4)

For if you forgive men when they sin against you, your Heavenly Father will also forgive you, but if you do not forgive men their sins, your Father will not forgive you. (Matt. 6:14-15)

Bear with each other and forgive whatever grievances you may have against one another. Forgive as the Lord forgave you. (Col. 3:13)

Sinner's Prayer

I know I am a sinner and have done many things that do not please You.
I need Your forgiveness today.

I believe that Jesus Christ is Your Son, and that You sent Him to be brutally beaten and
nailed to a cross to pay the penalty of my sins. Thank You for loving me that much.

I don't want to live in sinful ways anymore, so I am inviting Jesus Christ to come into my heart
and become my own personal Savior, to cleanse me from all the sins I have committed.

I need Your help to follow You and live for Jesus Christ the rest of my life.

Growing In God

- Talk to God every day and listen for His voice in your mind
- Read His Word
  (Begin in the book of John)
- Find a church that teaches God's Word and plug in
- Share your new faith in God with others

Lord, Please Forgive Me

Please write down the things you feel you need God to forgive you for.

I Need to truly forgive

Please write down the people you feel you need to try and forgive and for what.

I Need to Forgive Myself

Please write down the things you still feel guilty and shameful about. Give those things to Him.

BREAKING THE CHAIN

If you hold to My teaching, you are really My disciples.
Then you will know the truth and the truth will set you free!
(John 8:31–32)

SESSION TEN
Breaking The Chain
Discovering The REAL You

SESSION GOALS

- Recognize the positive things about you
- Define who God wants you to be
- Look at some of the positive things that may have come from the divorce of your parents
- Discover your spiritual gifts
- Discover what God's Word says about His children
- Learn about "Click Points"

The Lord is faithful to all His promises and loving toward all He has made. The Lord upholds all those who fall and lifts up all who are bowed down. The Lord is near to all who call on Him, to all who call on Him in truth; He hears their cry and saves them. —Ps. 145:14, 17-19

Freedom To Be Me

We often get buried by circumstances or others' expectations of us, and we can lose ourselves in the process. We can forget who we truly are and the kind of person we want to be.

Take some time to look at who *you* are: your strengths, weakness, likes, dislikes, your idea of fun, your goals, and so forth. Have fun with this!

The best thing about me is _____

_____

What I would like to improve about myself is _____

_____

What I like to do to have fun is _____

_____

What I like most about my looks is _____

_____

Do I make a good friend? _____ Why or why not? _____

_____

Not So Bad

Even though your parents' divorce was likely a painful experience as well as other ones, it is important to see the positive things that have come from even bad situations. As you travel the road to recovery, you will be surprised at how many good things have happened in your life as a result of damage you suffered as a kid. Please list them below.

Things I learned about myself through dealing with the divorce:

1.

2.

3.

4.

5.

New people/relationships in my life because of the divorce:

1.

2.

3.

4.

5.

Positive changes in me because of the divorce:

1.

2.

3.

4.

5.

Other good things that have happened because of the divorce:

1.

2.

3.

4.

5.

(Adapted from *The Big D... Divorce Thru the Eyes of a Teen*, by Krista Smith)

+ + *Pluses & Minuses* − −

It is good to realize that not all the changes we resist turn out negatively. Take some time and list some pluses and minuses that you have experienced because of your parents' divorce or other experiences. (Example: MINUS – had to do a lot of extra chores PLUS – Became a much more responsible person)

Pluses	Minuses

(Adapted from *The Big D... Divorce Thru the Eyes of a Teen*, by Krista Smith)

Spiritual Gifts

When someone gives you a wrapped gift, do you just let it lie on the table so you can look at it, or do you open it to see what is inside? We would all open it, right?

God has given you spiritual gifts that He wants you to open and use for His glory throughout your life. Check out this scripture:

Just as each of us has one body with many members, and these members do not all have the same function, so in Christ we who are many form one body, and each member belongs to all the others. We have different gifts, according to the grace given us. If a man's gift is prophesying, let him use it in proportion to his faith. If it is serving, let him serve; if it is teaching, let him teach, if it is encouraging, let him encourage, if it is contributing to the needs of others, let him give generously; if it is leadership, let him govern diligently, if it is showing mercy, let him do it cheerfully. (Rom. 12:4-8)

This is only a partial list of spiritual gifts. Others are found in I Corinthians 12 and you may find yours there. For now, please look at the list below and mark the one(s) that could be yours.

_____ HOSPITALITY—able to make people feel comfortable and welcome

_____ HELP—gives practical service

_____ LEADERSHIP—gives leadership and direction

_____ ADMINISTRATION—works behind the scenes to keep things in order

_____ COMPASSION/MERCY—shares a person's pain and struggles to provide support

_____ ENCOURAGEMENT—uses kind, encouraging words and actions freely

_____ SHOPPING (Just kidding!)

_____ DISCERNMENT—able to discern between right and wrong based on the Bible

_____ TEACHING—researches and teaches the Bible

_____ EXHORTATION—Encourages personal progress with honesty and openness

_____ GIVING—shares practical and material assistance

Which spiritual gifts do you presently use in serving the Lord? _____

_____

What gifts or abilities besides those mentioned here, do you see in yourself that God could use?

_____

_____

Identity Theft ... Who Am I Really?!

Many of us have defined ourselves by our circumstances, by who someone else told us we should be, or what society has told us. *Your self-image should come from who GOD says you are*, not from any human expectations. Explore the following verses and see how God designed you and values you. Be blessed!

John 1:12	I AM accepted ... I AM God's child
John 15:15	As a disciple, I am a FRIEND of Jesus Christ
Rom. 5:1	I have been JUSTIFIED
1 Cor. 6:17	I am united with the Lord, and I am ONE WITH Him in Spirit
1 Cor. 6:19-20	I have been bought with a price and I BELONG to God
1 Cor.12:27	I am a member of Christ's body
Eph. 1:3-8	I have been CHOSEN by God and ADOPTED as His child
Col. 1:13-14	I have been redeemed and forgiven of ALL my sins
Col. 2:9-10	I am COMPLETE in Christ
Heb. 4:14-16	I have DIRECT ACCESS to the throne of grace through Jesus Christ
Rom. 8:1-2	I am SECURE/I am FREE FROM CONDEMNATION
Rom. 8:28	I am ASSURED that God works for my good in ALL circumstances
Rom. 8:31-39	I am FREE from ANY condemnation brought against me, and I CANNOT be separated from the love of God
2 Cor. 1:21-22	I have been ESTABLISHED, ANOINTED, AND SEALED by God
Col. 3:1-4	I am hidden with Christ in God
Phil. 1:6	I am CONFIDENT that God WILL complete the good work He started in me
Phil. 3:20	I am a citizen of Heaven
2 Tim. 1:7	I have NOT been given a spirit of fear, but of POWER, LOVE, and a SOUND MIND
1 John 5:18	I am born of God, and the evil one CANNOT touch me
1 John 15:5	I am SIGNIFICANT/I am a branch of Jesus Christ, the True Vine and channel of His life
John 15:16	I have been CHOSEN AND APPOINTED to bear fruit
1 Cor. 3:16	I AM God's temple
2 Cor. 5:17-21	I am a minister of reconciliation for God
Eph. 2:6	I am seated WITH Jesus Christ in the heavenly realm
Eph. 2:10	I AM God's workmanship
Eph. 3:12	I may approach God with FREEDOM AND CONFIDENCE
Phil. 4:13	I CAN do ALL things through Christ, Who strengthens me

(Adapted from *Victory over the Darkness*, by Dr. Neil Anderson)

Now, *this* is the real you! This is the truth about you; not the enemy's lies and faulty thinking you have been dragging through life. Who will you listen to now?

LOVE LINKS
LOVE & RELATIONSHIPS

LOVE...bears all things, believes all things, hopes all things, endures all things. Love NEVER fails.
1 Corinthians 1:13

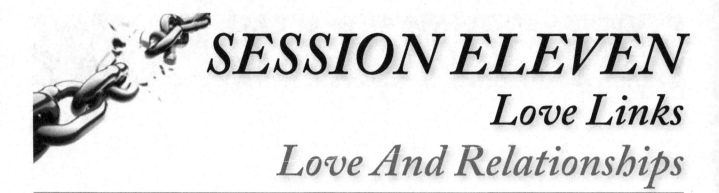

SESSION ELEVEN
Love Links
Love And Relationships

SESSION GOALS

- Explore your thoughts and attitudes about a love relationship
- Learn about trust and respect in a healthy marriage
- Reflect on your family patterns and beliefs about vows and commitment
- Learn healthier ways to deal with conflict and confrontations
- Explore what God's Word says about love

Love is patient, love is kind and is not jealous; love does not brag and is not arrogant, does not act unbecoming; it does not seek its own, is not provoked, does not take into account a wrong suffered. It does not rejoice in unrighteousness, but rejoices with the truth. — 1 Corinthians 13:4-6

All You Need Is Love, Right?

We were made for relationships, romantic or not. You may have seen great long-term marriages in addition to seeing your parents' and others' marriages break up, so you may be confused as to what love and marriage are really all about—and why the Lord created them.

Please explore your thoughts, ideas and your understanding about what true love is all about on the page below.

Describe in one sentence what *love* is: _____

_____

_____

Describe in one sentence what *marriage* is: _____

_____

_____

What are two of the most important elements of a healthy marriage?

1. _____

2. _____

What is your understanding of what vows mean in a wedding ceremony (for example, for better or worse, richer or poorer, sickness or health, forsaking all others as long as we both shall live)? _____

_____

_____

_____

Is it easy for you to tell others you love them? _____

Why or why not? _____

_____

Because of your parents' divorce or other influences, what are some of the fears (e.g., mistrust, insecurity, infidelity, fear of abandonment, fear of failure, and so forth) you have about being married?

_____

_____

_____

Do you believe that love truly can last forever and that you can have a healthy marriage? _____

Why or why not? _____

_____

_____

_____

What do you think it means to "live as one" in marriage? _____

_____

_____

_____

_____

_____

Vows, Promises, and Commitment

Do you feel as if you let people down a lot? Do friends, family, and others get frustrated when you promise something and can't deliver? Do you find that you would rather walk away than make a strong commitment to a relationship?

Most children of divorce struggle with all these issues. After all, what did their parents' wedding vows mean, anyway? What is the big deal with commitment?

Please answer the questions below to explore these subjects and explain how you think your parents' divorce or other experiences have affected certain areas of your life. Please be specific.

When asked to make a commitment, what stops you? _____

_____

_____

When did others, besides your parents, break a commitment, promise, or vow to you? Write about as many as you want to.

_____

_____

How do you think these have affected you? _____

_____

_____

Are you usually late for things? _____ If so, think deeply and explain why you think that is: _____

_____

_____

How loyal of a person are you? What challenges do you face in being loyal?

_____

_____

_____

_____

Explain what you believe integrity means: _____

_____

_____

Do you believe you are a person of integrity? _____

Would friends say you are? _____

Would your employer say you are? _____

Would your family say you are? _____

Would your children and/or grandchildren say you are? _____

Would God say you are? _____

What is a vow/promise you have kept in your life—and to whom? _____

_____

What is a vow/promise you have broken in your life—and to whom? _____

_____

> When a man makes a vow to the Lord or takes an oath to obligate himself by a
> pledge, he must not break his word but must do everything he said.
> —Num. 30:2

What steps do you need to take to become more of a trustworthy person? _____

_____

_____

Conflict, Tensions, and Confrontation

There are many ways to face conflict; some are effective for resolving the issues, and some are not. Below is a list concerning what kind of example you had as a child growing up as well as some tools to help.

1.   The general way to handle conflict in our home was:

_____ Yelling, screaming, cussing

_____ Hitting, slapping, and so forth

_____ Ignoring the situation/other person

_____ Sitting down and talking it out

_____ Talking to someone else about it instead of the person you had the conflict with

_____ Usually a lecture by a parent

_____ Usually grounded

_____ Other _____

_____

Some families are good at conflict resolution, and some are not. It depends on the communication skills in the family, whether there are addictions involved, the age of the children, and the level of good parenting skills, among other things.

This is an important area of family patterns and shows how they are passed on from generation to generation. If your parents had parents who yelled, screamed, and cussed, chances are they did the same thing in your home. If they had parents who communicated well and were willing to work out resolutions, then chances are you had that type of home growing up.

Once a pattern has been set, it can be very difficult to break that pattern. This may result in you not being excited to be a parent, whether now or in the future. You may not want your kids to grow up with the same "stuff" you did. Right?

We are here to tell you that you can certainly break patterns of verbal or physical abuse in your family if you are willing to do the work.

Here are some ways to improve the way you resolve conflicts.

STEP ONE—Realize that there will always be differences of opinion. There are always two sides to a conflict. Each person has a right to an opinion, and it is important to look at what is behind behavior.

Note: It is important to take time to pray about it; a peaceful and helpful resolution is possible with God's guidance.

Note: If you are so upset that you can't talk without angrily hurting the other person or damaging your relationship, you can take a step back and return later to discuss the issue when both of you have calmed down. During the time out, take deep breaths and ask God to help you accomplish a positive outcome.

STEP TWO—Make up your mind that you are working for a resolution—not to control or get your way or to prove that you are right. Do what you can to avoid a competition of wills. Have a positive purpose.

STEP THREE—Resolve in your mind that you are going to exercise patience and kindness; that the louder the other person gets, the quieter you will be, that you will not fuel the conflict, and that you are an adult and will control yourself.

STEP FOUR—Learn to listen and *truly hear* what the other is trying to say. Don't think about what you are going to say next; listen *fully* to the other person and don't interrupt. Keep a check on your facial expressions as well. The more you listen, the more you will learn.

STEP FIVE—When you speak, keep your voice calm but firm. Stay away from using "always" or "never." (For example: "You *always* forget to lock the door" or "You *never* do anything around here.") Such statements are not true and only put the other person on the defensive. If the other person interrupts you, stop talking and remind him that you didn't interrupt when he was speaking, stating that you would like to finish. Tell him you are interested in what he has to say.

STEP SIX—When both of you have given your opinions, thoughts and concerns, it is time to figure out how to resolve the conflict. After hearing each other, can you see what would be the best solution? Remember that this is not about getting your way or being in control but about resolving a conflict peacefully and keeping a strong, loving relationship in the process.

STEP SEVEN— If you need to, write down what each of you say you will do to make the necessary adjustments, ask for forgiveness, forgive each other, and if both feel comfortable, hug and make up. If possible and both agree, close the confrontation in prayer and ask the Lord to heal hurt feelings and restore your relationship.

Note: This type of process will no doubt take a longer amount of time and may feel awkward at first, but the result should be a lot better than just flying off the handle and hurting one another and accomplishing nothing.

Do not repay anyone evil for evil. Be careful to do what is right in the eyes of everybody. If it is possible,
as far as it depends on you, live at peace with everyone [including your spouse and children].
—Rom. 12:17-18

Chained No More

Trust and Respect

Love can mean many things to many people. It can mean a romantic dinner, caring for each other when sick, a night of passion, or just staring at the sunset together. What does the word *love* mean to *you*?

The basis for love, I believe, is trust and respect, and love becomes the result of that. If you don't have both of these elements in your love relationship, it can become more of an obligation; an existence. Take your time to read the important elements of a godly marriage. Remember that this is the ideal and something to shoot for.

TELL THE TRUTH: This is one of the most important elements to a healthy relationship. When someone lies to you or is unfaithful to you, from that moment on, your trust is lessened. What do you know you can believe? If you lied once, you can lie again, and then trust is broken. God's Word is strong about honesty and integrity. We are not children anymore, trying to get away with things; we are adults. We appreciate people being truthful with us, and we should do the same. How can I believe you are committed to me and love me if I can't trust you with simple truth?

RESPECT EACH OTHER'S PRIVACY: We do not own each other and should never treat the other person as a possession. Both should be able to have their privacy about their pasts, personal habits, and things they enjoy away from you. Now, if there is something the other person is doing that is hurting the marriage (pornography, an affair, or other hurtful actions past or present), take the time to discuss it calmly and try to resolve it together.

UNDERSTAND: We don't always know what is behind what someone tells us, do we? Try to understand why the other person is hurting and find out the "whys behind the whats". Figure out why he/she does certain things or has certain issues by observing and then asking in a nonthreatening way. Both people have the right to think and do what they want to, within reason. You may never completely understand, but love him/her enough to try.

SERVE EACH OTHER: God commands us to serve one another, which does not mean that one becomes a servant, so to speak. Serving one another means trying to think ahead about what the other person may need and how you can help. This does not mean the other person is helpless; it is just another form of loving her. This does not include keeping score about who is doing more or who cleaned it the last time. There is no room for this type of competition in marriage! Serve with love and care and full commitment to your marriage.

TRACK RECORD: It is important to know the track record of the other person. Is he a person of integrity, kindness, strong character, monogamous, honest, and so forth? If you doubt his intentions, has he given you a reason for that, or were you hurt by someone else in that area? Don't let this person pay for another person's issue. If there are issues that are difficult to get over and you see a pattern that is hurting your relationship, suggest going to a counselor or pastor. It's worth it.

REMOVE DISRESPECT OF ANY KIND: The words we use can hurt someone deeply, so avoid all putdowns, cussing, and calling each other bad names in your marriage. The Bible is full of scriptures telling us how we should treat each other. Respect each other's privacy, differences of ideas, and ways of doing things—and definitely don't disrespect the other's parenting, especially in front of your children. Never disrespect your spouse in front of others, even in jest. It only makes you look bad, and it is hurtful to your spouse and damaging to your marriage.

ETCH THE WORD OF GOD ON YOUR RELATIONSHIP: Make time in God's Word one of your priorities as a couple. Attend church together and get involved with people who are in healthy relationships so you can encourage one another in your marriage commitments. Make the time to pray for one another and with each other. Bring big decisions before the Lord together and ask for His guidance as a couple. Play worship music in your home and car and attend good concerts; there are many different styles for all tastes. Enjoy your walk with the Lord together and permeate your relationship with Him.

STAND UP FOR EACH OTHER: Make sure you always have the other's back. No matter what the conflict, stand up for each other in front of others and question/confront behind closed doors. Assume your spouse is in the right unless you find out otherwise and never let your spouse feel as if he/she is alone, with no one to walk beside her and defend her.

PUT COMPETITION ASIDE: Nothing can hurt a marriage more or quicker than arguments and competition. If you have to win, then you are both losers. Consider that you are trying to win an argument and want to prove that you are right. You are purposely working to prove that your spouse is wrong, and therefore you both lose. Love is not about that. It is about working together, encouraging one another in love. Next time, learn to listen and try to work together for understanding and a compromise, even if it means you agree to disagree. Now kiss and make up!

ENCOURAGE ONE ANOTHER: You may have not seen your parents encourage each other, and you may have been witness to a lot of shouting and violence. Obviously, that is not the way to treat someone you said marriage vows to, right? You know how it feels to be encouraged, so give a lot of it to the one you love. Look for the things that are positive about him and let him know you appreciate him. If he is headed toward a better job, school, or another accomplishment, encourage him and help him achieve his goals. When he reaches a big goal, celebrate with him and let him know how proud you are of him. When he falls, lift him up with your words and actions.

COUPLE TIME: Our world is fast-paced, and many times couples are like ships passing in the night. Intimacy fits in the schedule rarely and can become unfulfilling. Make efforts to end the evenings alone, giving you time to talk and cuddle before going to bed. Turn the TV/computer/cell phone off, take a walk, or sit on the couch and reconnect. Once a year, at least, plan a weekend away to have some time alone to enjoy each other with no distractions. Meet for lunch once a week, if possible, to connect during the week. Meet in a park, a restaurant, a mall food court ... It doesn't matter. Have fun dating again. Note: Don't assume there will be intimacy when there is conflict. Work on the conflict first.

TAKE TIME TO REALLY LISTEN: There is so much noise around us, so many distractions, and so little time to communicate face-to-face. When your spouse is sharing something, face her, stop what you are doing, and listen without thinking about what you are going to say when she takes a breath! Hear what is behind the hurt if she is sharing something that is burdening her. You don't always need to give advice; in fact, only give it if she asks. Try it. Sometimes people just need to vent and don't need you to "fix" them. Just walk beside them in love.

What elements need to be improved in your present relationship? _____

Which ones were missing in your past relationships? _____

Do you see a pattern?_____

Extra Hints To Keep The Peace

HINT #1—Keep the main thing the main thing. When you are discussing an issue, *do not* bring up other issues from the past. If you haven't resolved a past issue, try to find another time to do that. Don't keep score by bringing up past offenses.

HINT #2—Remember that you made a *covenant*, not merely a paper contract, with your spouse at the wedding. You also made a covenant to God on that day. How does that affect your commitment?

HINT #3—If you and your spouse cannot resolve issues, be willing to get some guidance from a mediator, pastor, marriage counselor, or therapist. If your spouse refuses to go, be willing to go alone. Value your spouse and your marriage enough to do the work to make it work.

HINT #4—If there is a conflict, ask yourself if it is worth the relationship. Pick your battles, compromise when you can, and always be willing to apologize and genuinely ask for forgiveness if you have offended your spouse. Give grace unconditionally.

HINT #5—Pray daily for your marriage, your spouse and that you will be the spouse God wants you to be.

Love And Gods' Word

Please look at the following scriptures and tell how you think they can apply to marriage:

Be completely humble and gentle; be patient, bearing with one another in love. (Eph. 4:2)	
Speaking the truth in love, we will in all things grow up into Him who is the Head, that is Christ. (Eph. 4:15)	
Be imitators of God, therefore, as dearly loved children, and live a life of love, just as Christ loved us. (Eph. 5:1-2)	
Serve one another in love. (Gal. 5:13)	
Whatever you do, work at it with all your heart, as working for the Lord, not for men ... (Col. 3:23)	
Bear with each other and forgive whatever grievances you may have against one another. (Col. 3:13)	
A gentle answer turns away wrath, but a harsh word stirs up anger (Prov. 15:1).	
Pride goes before destruction, a haughty spirit before a fall. (Prov. 16:18)	

MAKING A NEW CHAIN
(Part One)

...ONE LINK AT A TIME

SESSION TWELVE
Making A New Chain (Part One)
Changing Old Patterns

 **SESSION GOALS**

- Realize your old patterns of thoughts and behavior
- Examine who you are and who you want to become
- Reflect on the influences you have in your life and how they may be affecting you
- Allow yourself to look at your dreams for the future and explore ways to achieve them

Do not conform any longer to the patterns of this world, but be transformed by the renewing of your mind. Then you will be able to test and approve what God's will is ... His good, pleasing and perfect will. (Rom. 12:2)

What's On Your Mind?

Our society is full of distractions through the media, television, magazines, computer screens, music, and movies. Our minds can be overloaded with things that cloud what God has in mind for us. Using this page, explore what is on your mind.

Indicate the activities and influences you have in your life and how they may be affecting your mind.

"As a man thinketh in his heart, so is he." Proverbs 23:7 (KJV)

Favorite TV shows _____
Positive influence _____
Possible negative influence _____

Movies watched _____
Positive influence _____
Possible negative influence _____

Magazines you read _____
Positive influence _____
Possible negative influence _____

Music you listen _____
Positive influence _____
Possible negative influence _____

Computer websites _____
Positive influence _____
Possible negative influence _____

Books you read _____
Positive influence _____
Possible negative influence _____

Friends you hang out with _____
Positive influence _____
Possible negative influence _____

Free-time activities _____
Positive influence _____
Possible negative influence _____

*Whatever is **noble**, whatever is **right**, whatever is **pure**, whatever is **lovely**, whatever is **admirable** ...*
*If anything is **excellent** or **praiseworthy**, **think on these things**. —Phil. 4:8*

What changes do you need to make in the above areas of influence (ie. eliminate violent movies that may feed your anger)?

Looking In The Mirror

Anyone who listens to the Word but does not do what it says is like a man who looks at his face in a mirror and, after looking at himself, goes away and immediately forgets what he looks like. (James 1:22-24)

Now we see but a poor reflection as in a mirror; then [when we get to heaven]) we shall see God face to face. (1 Cor. 13:12)

We, who with unveiled faces all reflect the Lord's glory, are being transformed into His likeness with ever-increasing glory, which comes from the Lord Who is the Spirit. (2 Cor. 3:18)

Take some time to look at yourself in a mirror. Look beyond the image you see to the person you are.

What do you see in the mirror? Look deeper. What do you see that you like?

What do you see that you don't like?

What do you *want* to see in the mirror?

What are you willing to do to get there?

In A Perfect World

Think for a moment about how you would like your life to look in five years. Write or draw that in this space.

In this space, write the things that will help you get there. Also write about what could hold you back from that dream.

MAKING A NEW CHAIN

(Part Two)

...ONE LINK AT A TIME

SESSION THIRTEEN
Making A New Chain (Part Two)
Developing New Patterns

SESSION GOALS

- Examine the subject of change, how to truly attain it in areas of your life with God's help, and move forward in freedom, chained no more
- Reflect on the areas that need to be built up in the future and strategize about how you will make those changes

Do not conform any longer to the patterns of this world, but be transformed by the renewing of your mind, Then you will be able to test and approve what God's will is—His good, pleasing and perfect will. —Rom. 12:2

Change

The first step toward *change* is awareness.
The second step is *acceptance*.
The third step is *action*.

At the beginning of this book, on page 61, "Links of Issues," you checked the issues that you see in yourself. Awareness of these issues is the first step toward healing. We have addressed most of them throughout the past twelve chapters. Facing those issues, seeing where they began, and learning how God can heal them has hopefully led you toward a much healthier and brighter future.

The last two chapters of *Chained No More* will give you practical tools to put into action what God has shown you.

My son, do not forget my teaching, but keep my commands in your heart, for they will prolong your life many years and bring you prosperity. Let love and faithfulness never leave you; bind them around your neck, write them on the tablet of your heart. Then you will win favor and a good name in the sight of God and man. Trust in the Lord with all your heart and lean not on your own understanding. In all your ways acknowledge Him and He will make your paths straight.
(Proverbs 3:1-6)

Steps to Change

KNOW THE INFORMATION—Become a student of God's Word, the Bible. Take the time to understand and absorb it.

MEMORIZATION—It is important not to just read the Bible but also to make it part of your thinking by memorizing scripture. Find a method that will make it easy for you.

MEDITATION—The process of working biblical truth over and over in the mind so you can gain deeper insight into its meaning.

IMAGINATION—Picture yourself living the changes you need to make and consider how you can be a different person.

APPLICATION—Make the change and purposely do it every single day. Say in strength, "I will *choose* to change."

"Change your mind and transform your life!"
—"A Mind Renewed by God" written by Dr. Kimball Hodge

Rebuilding Your Life

You have gone through many weeks of evaluating your life and exploring the effects that the divorce of your parents and other painful experiences had on you as an adult. You have looked at God's love for you and how much He values you. You have hopefully learned about His forgiveness and His grace on a deeper level.

Now is the time to begin building new "links" toward a brighter and healthier future. Please indicate the following areas you want to rebuild in your life.

_____ My ability to trust people

_____ Being able to make a commitment and stick with it

_____ Not feeling as if I am on the outside looking in

_____ Not being so afraid of being rejected by others

_____ Learning how to control my anger

_____ Learning how to have a closer walk with Jesus Christ

_____ Being able to truly forgive someone and move on

_____ Building my confidence/understanding my worth

_____ Learning not to compare myself to others but to see my own value and theirs

_____ Learning not to let my emotions rule me or cloud my good judgment

Other areas _____

_____

_____

Rebuilding Your Life: Workpage

On the previous page, you checked the areas that you want to rebuild in your life. Now, please consider all of those areas and write out ways you are going to help make them happen and what you are willing to do. Following that, write down the benefits you hope to see because of your efforts. Please put a lot of thought into this as you strategize.

ISSUE #1 _____

WHAT YOU ARE GOING TO DO _____

_____

_____

_____

BENEFITS _____

_____

_____

_____

ISSUE #2 _____

WHAT YOU ARE GOING TO DO _____

_____

_____

_____

BENEFITS _____

_____

_____

ISSUE #3 _____

WHAT YOU ARE GOING TO DO _____

_____

_____

BENEFITS _____

_____

_____

ISSUE #4 _____

WHAT YOU ARE GOING TO DO _____

_____

_____

BENEFITS _____

_____

_____

ISSUE #5 _____

WHAT YOU ARE GOING TO DO _____

_____

_____

BENEFITS _____

_____

_____

Links Learned

Please write some of the things you learned in *Chained No More*, and how you hope they will affect your life now.

Putting Feet To Your Prayers

We can pray all day and wait for God to answer without doing our part and taking the necessary steps with His leading. Example: praying for a better job but not getting out there and interviewing. Or praying that God will give you an A on your exam, but not studying for it.

What are some prayer requests you have asked God about lately, and how have you done your part? List them below.

REQUEST:_____

_____

MY PART:_____

_____

REQUEST:_____

_____

MY PART:_____

_____

REQUEST:_____

_____

MY PART:_____

_____

REQUEST:_____

_____

MY PART:_____

_____

CONGRATULATIONS! YOU DID IT!

> We hope you have benefitted from *Chained No More*, and that God has done a mighty work in you over the last few months.
>
> We pray you can move forward in your faith, in strength, knowing that the Holy Spirit is there to guide you toward a much brighter and healthier future.
>
> *May God bless you with His joy!*

"Chained No More" Debrief Form

NAME _____ **AGE** _____

ADDRESS _____ **EMAIL** _____

On a scale of 1-10, how helpful did you find *Chained No More*? _____

What was the most effective part? _____

Why? _____

_____

What was the least effective? _____

Why? _____

_____

On a scale of 1-10, please rate the following:

Effective and thought-provoking questions (_____) _____

Spiritual emphasis (_____) _____

Practical tools for future success in life (_____) _____

Effective healing and growth (_____) _____

Please comment and give suggestions below so we can continue to improve this program for effectiveness and success. Thank you for your input and for participating in *Chained No More*.

NOTE: Upon completing this form, please tear it out and send it to: Robyn B Ministries   P.O. Box 71726   Springfield, OR 97475

CREDITS AND RESOURCES

CONTRIBUTORS:

Elsa Colopy, speaker and author (www.elsakokcolopy.com)—Colorado Springs, Colorado

Pastor Colin Halstead, MA therapist, pastor of Renewal Ministries at First
Baptist Church of Eugene—Eugene, Oregon (colinh@fbceugene.com)

Dr. Kimball Hodge III, D. Min. pastor and author—Central Point, Oregon

Linda Ranson-Jacobs, speaker, writer, and developer of *Divorce Care for Kids (hlp4.com)*
—Navarre, Florida

Dr. Marlin Schultz, D.Min., marriage/family therapist—Eugene, Oregon

Krista Smith, Developer of *The Big D...Divorce Thru the Eyes of a Teen*
—Big Lake, Minnesota (sonsetpointministries.com)

Many people interviewed are adult children of divorce, willing to share their stories
and the many effects that their parents' divorce had on their lives.

Most importantly, the Lord God, His guidance in writing this material,
and whose Word is the best contribution of all.

RESOURCE MATERIALS:

The Bible—God's Word

Between Two Worlds by Elizabeth Marquardt, Three Rivers Press, 2005

A Mind Renewed by God by Dr. Kimball Hodge III, Harvest House Publishers, 1998
(kimlyndahodge@gmail.com)

The Big D...Divorce Thru the Eyes of a Teen, by Krista Smith, AMFM Press, 2010
(sonsetpointministries.com)

Divorce Care for Kids by Linda Jacobs, Church Initiative, 2004 (hlp4.com)

Adult Children of Divorce by Jim Conway InterVarsity Press, 1990